WHAT PEOPLE ARE SAYING . . .

"Peter Engler's non-traditional approach to job search is based on his thirty years of business experience, six years as a retained executive recruiter, and eight years as a career strategist and coach. He has worked with people of all ages around the country helping them achieve career success. This isn't just ordinary career advice...it's extraordinary career advice." — **Eric Wentworth, author of** *A Plan for Life: The 21st Century Guide to Success in Health, Wealth, Career, Education, Love, Place...and You*!

"Peter Engler is an experienced business professional, executive recruiter and veteran career strategist who has laid out an effective plan to determine what you really want to do, how to build an action plan, and how to take on a proactive job, and career, search. His often non-traditional approaches to this important life task make this book even more unique and valuable for people of all ages and in all professions. Peter has been a long-time friend and mentor who's given me valuable guidance over the years as my career evolved." — **Ted Prodromou, Award-winning author of** *Ultimate Guide to LinkedIn for Business and Ultimate Guide to Twitter for Business*

"Looking for work can often be a stressful and frustrating experience, but it doesn't have to be that way. Peter Engler's book, *Your Crystal Clear Career Path*, offers exceptional guidance to help you find the right opportunities, create powerful resumés, and have successful interviews that can lead to rewarding work. He takes a holistic approach to career planning. This involves completing a deep assessment of your personal goals and abilities (understand who you are and what really you want), an action plan with exercises to guide you, and an execution strategy to reach the companies that are a good fit. By following this process, reading his real-world examples of people who successfully approached different opportunities, and completing the exercises included in the book, you can go through the phases of your career journey with confidence. It's like having your own personal career coach with you at all times. Engler's outstanding advice applies to people in many industries and job levels – from those just starting out in their careers to people making career transitions at age 50 and beyond." — **Linda Donovan, Author,** *Tech Grief: Survive and Thrive Through Career Losses*

"Peter Engler has synthesized his own careers as a marketing executive, executive recruiter and career coach into an inspiring book for those looking for the job they deserve. With great wisdom he provides both big ideas and important tidbits to guide and motivate the job seeker. It's particularly well-suited for the experienced candidate." — **David Pilati, PhD, veteran executive coach and retained recruiter**

"Peter has captured a roadmap to searching and determining a career and job agenda. To be a great colleague and employee, one must like what they do, who they do it for, and where they do it. Along the path, find a rabbi or priest (mentor), who will share with you all the things you don't want to hear." — **Paul Dinovitz, Executive Director of Hearst Foundations**

Your Crystal Clear Career Path

Featuring Smart, New and Effective Job Search Strategies

Find Rewarding Work, Not Just a Job!

Peter G. Engler

Career Strategist & Coach

Grantham Press

BELVEDERE, CALIFORNIA

56 Bayview Avenue
Belvedere, California 94920
granthampress.com
415-601-2444

Cover Design: Matt Hinrichs
Editing, Layout and Book Production: Ruth Schwartz
Operations Director and Proofreader: Carole Engler

Your Crystal Clear Career Path/ Peter G. Engler. 1st ed.
ISBN: 978-0-9894850-3-6
Library of Congress Control Number: 2014912421

This book is dedicated to you and everyone you know who is seeking their true career direction and resultant professional and personal happiness and bounty

I want to thank my hundreds of clients, young, middle-aged and older who worked smart and hard with my guidance to find new jobs, new careers, and new experiences in the process.

And, perhaps, their stories and this book will help you create your story of heightened self-knowledge, sense of purpose and action, and realized goals and happiness.

APPRECIATION

This book is in appreciation for the hundreds of young, middle-aged and "mature" clients who have engaged me to help guide them through the labyrinth of career searches. Their interest, integrity, trust and enthusiasm for the process and the results have been very heartening and extremely rewarding. As they say, "the devil is in the details" and your success is in addressing those details and doing the work.

I hope you glean at least one new idea that serves you well in your own search for a career that is responsive to you and your goals — something that inspires you to increase your efforts to obtain the right job, at the right company for you.

Also, many thanks to the numerous people who have provided insights and comments on this book. No one has all the answers, surely not your author.

Special thanks to my wife, Carole, for proofing and advising on various aspects of the book including the always challenging chore of selecting a title; to my sons, Rob, Scott and Jeremy for forging successful and interesting careers, and to Ruth Schwartz for editing, book layout and production. Big thanks to Alexandria Zech, Peyton Stein, Eric and Carol Ann Wentworth, Christine Konkal, Monika and Jan Zands, Linda Donovan, Ted Prodromou, Gordon Dupries, Jesse Gros, Gary White, Dino Dinowitz, Susan Kearny, Andrew Dun, David Pilati, Avery Mann and others for their careful review of and comments on the book's direction and content, and to you the reader, for deciding to buy it and use it to guide you on your Crystal Clear Career Path!

Like everything in life, this is a work of collaboration, and is much the better for that.

Peter Engler
June 2014

TABLE OF CONTENTS

Introduction

This book is the result of twenty years in major advertising agencies and corporations in New York and San Francisco, ten years as a San Francisco retained executive recruiter, two years directing a senior executive outplacement program at Right Management, and as a Career Strategist and Coach in my own practice since 2004 with the Engler Career Group (englercareergroup.com).

The book's earnest purpose is to help you design, create and move along your crystal clear career path, and contains many tried and true, as well as new and effective, job search strategies to help you enjoy a fun, profitable and satisfying career.

While this book is primarily addressed to men and women 45 and older, most of the advice and tactics are totally applicable to college grads and people in their thirties.

The book contains the following key types of information:

A complete program to help you define your career goals and get the job you deserve. I have provided a time-tested step-by-step guide to better understanding yourself, creating powerful resumés, bios and other job search tools, and then taking action on all of this in a proactive job and career search.

Articles that I have written for various organizations with a focus on "non-traditional" career guidance. They are my views and insights, and I hope they help you think way outside the box during your search.

In addition there are some stories to encourage, enlighten and enthuse you woven throughout Part 1. These are only a few of the many stories that I have enjoyed being a part of. They are evidence that, with a solid assessment of your personality, interests, needs, talents and goals, coupled with the development of a winning set of career search tools, that you *can* achieve career success and satisfaction.

These are examples of actual client's experiences, which hopefully will give you a "real world" feel for how different people have used these principles and practices to pursue their personal and professional goals. I have masked their names for privacy purposes, but their stories are ones they would be glad to tell you.

A proactive search is the operative term here; it means you analyze, initiate and follow-through on everything that looks like it fits in your search plan. It does not mean that you depend solely on headhunters, business associates, the Safeway checkout lady or anyone else with job tips. Your job is to take the *lead* on your job search and *actively manage* and improve your career.

Your goal, I believe, is to find the job that is *right* for you, where you are *right* for the company (them), and that combination is *right* for your long-term career success.

No one can do this for you. No coach, no friend, no associate. Not even your spouse or your old boss. Only you can do the three parts: know yourself, build your action tools and execute your action plan to achieve success.

Only you — with a little help from all of these people, of course. By implementing the strategies described in this book, you can create your own crystal clear career path, and ultimately find the work that is the best fit for you, your talents and the company's needs.

Who Am I...Really?
What Do I Want?
Where Should I Go?
When? How?

Clarity is key to your success.
— Anonymous

As a retained executive recruiter, I found that most candidates, most of whom were very successful, did not have their job search act together. They did not know the job search drill and assumed that my role was to find them a job. They did not have very good resumés, had not prepared for the interview and were often not very clear on why they deserved to be considered for the opportunity.

I was surprised to learn that this was the rule, not the exception. Most people did not know how to find a job because for the first time, they had to actually pursue jobs rather than answer calls from headhunters and read job postings.

Think about it. In the eighties and nineties, you did not have to go after jobs; they came to you for the most part. You took the best job that was offered even though it might not be ideal. If it paid well, offered certain benefits and was in an area of general interest, you grabbed it and jumped in. You were in a *reactive career environment* where others (your uncle, the persuasive HR executive, your buddies) most likely made your job decisions for you.

Today, jobs don't "show up" like they used to. And today, you should be much more discriminating regarding which jobs are best for you. At 35, 45 or 55 years of age, you cannot afford to take on something that is not going to reward, energize and satisfy you.

But, how do you know what is best for you if you do not do the homework?

Times have changed, and I believe that executives had better change as well. The need to carefully and intelligently nurture your career is even more true today than before. Jobs are scarce; good jobs are even more rare.

This rampant "career confusion" was the basis for my decision to become a Career Strategist and Coach. I believed that I could help men and women of all ages build a stronger, more powerful and more persuasive candidacy based upon career clarity, resulting in their finding the *right work, not just a job.*

Over the last twelve years, I have distilled an effective career search into three distinct phases:

Phase One: A deep and honest **Assessment** to determine exactly who you are, where you should focus your energies, and what jobs and companies make sense for you.

Phase Two: A complete and powerful **Action Plan** to provide you with the best tools (resumé, bio, 60-second elevator speech, interviewing skills, outreach skills, LinkedIn training, etc.) to successfully obtain that "right job for you."

Phase Three: GO FOR IT — Implement your Action Plan, ensuring that you are doing the right things every day, whether employed or un-employed, to build and manage your career to its fullest extent.

If you do not fully know yourself and your goals, have a strong **Action Plan** in place and are not taking daily steps to execute that plan, then you are simply missing the boat and treading water.

Working through these three important phases is what this book is about, and hopefully this critical mission makes sense to you.

CHAPTER 1

A Three-Phase Career Clarity Process

Life isn't about finding yourself, it is about creating yourself.
— George Bernard Shaw

This three-phase program is designed to prepare and arm you as you successfully pursue the right job for you, at the right company for you.

I have employed this **three-part Career Clarity Process** for years, focusing on the three key phases of a successful career search; **Personal Assessment, Action Plan Development** and **Action Plan Execution**.

The first phase, **Assessment,** includes a rare opportunity for you to think deeply about yourself: your true interests, desires, experiences, both good and bad, where you want to live, what you really like doing and with whom you most enjoy working. This is a chance to drill down in your mind and conduct a thoughtful inventory of yourself.

This phase also contains a professional personality assessment, **The Birkman Method®**, which helps you understand three key things about yourself; how you are *perceived by others*, what your primary *interests* are and what are your key *needs*. Most surveys only provide information on your general behavior — the first item. The Birkman provides important additional insights into the "why" of you — what captures your attention and energy and what factors have to be present in your life, job and activities for you to be successful and happy.

As you will learn in the next chapter, I also have my clients complete a personal **Mission Statement** as well as a "**Bridges and Barriers**" document.

The second phase, **Action Plan Development**, is designed to re-build your career search tools so they have more impact and strength. You will write your **Communications Platform**, the same document used by advertising agencies to create winning commercials. You then create new resumés and bios that tell your story with more uniqueness and impact, causing prospective employers and networking contacts to "want to meet you." You also create more memorable 60-second elevator speeches, emails, voicemails and other tools that you can use to gain access to key people at key companies. You will learn how to get interviews, how to interview with confidence and impact, and how to follow-up to keep your candidacy vibrant. You, in brief, learn how to better promote yourself.

An older man, pushing sixty, Ben had many years of experience as an operations executive at several law firms. Keenly sensitive to his age, he had lost confidence that he could find new employment. One of the things he enjoyed doing was beekeeping. We included this in his bio and resumé, and he found in subsequent interviews, that everyone was very interested in his bee-keeping avocation and spent little time worrying about his age or anything else. He was hired for probably the best job he had won to date, and contributed to a major shift in how the new law firm managed their profitability.

The third phase, **Action Plan Execution**, is just that: working every day to find not just a job, but the *right work* for you. You will create your most important tool, your **Target Company List**. This contains the 10-15 companies within a 45-minute commute of your home, that are the "right companies" for you based upon who you are, who they are and who they need. Making this match is what makes for a successful job search and more importantly, a successful and happy career.

Ted is a 34-year-old father of two boys who has a great job at a major winery in the Napa Valley. The problem is that, while it is a highly-sought position among young people, it does not satisfy his need to work more closely with agricultural products, especially organic free market foods and beverages. So, while continuing to do his job well, he is identifying and networking with regional food producers with fallow land who might be interested in gaining experience in this new consumer products arena under his guidance. To gain their interest, I am guiding him to contact people who could help his search, having him use precise emails and smart follow-up call procedures. The exciting aspect of this evolution is that Ted is much more excited and upbeat about his prospects, now that he has a formal and organized set of search tools including a bright resumé and a very intriguing bio that causes people to want to meet him.

Here's a related story that not only demonstrates the power of getting clear about your target companies, but also the power of networking:

Alan is a 55-year-old executive in a major consumer foods company in Chicago. Interestingly, he has come to know Ted through my auspices as they share common goals. He, too, wants to shift his career more directly to solving the financial challenges represented by Organic Sustainable Food Marketing and has dialogued with Ted in this regard. A perfect example of mutually valuable networking, Alan and Ted are likely to learn from each and benefit from this informal association.

CHAPTER 2

Phase One: Personal and Career Assessment — Who Am I?

The only person you are destined to become is the person you decide to be.
— Ralph Waldo Emerson

Every journey begins with deciding who you are and what you want to accomplish. Knowing yourself, your needs, interests, experience, knowledge and other factors is helpful when you are contemplating a major trip, say to Europe or Asia. You review all the literature, get input from friends, websites and travel agents, determine costs and schedules and begin to plan your trip. You then execute the plan; you go on the much-awaited trip and enjoy the fruits of your investigation and planning.

The same is true for contemplating and charting your career. You must truly know yourself, something that most people think they do — when research shows that this just isn't true. I saw evidence of this when executives would undertake a 360-degree personality evaluation of themselves. They first evaluated themselves on various attributes, and then had associates *who they selected* conduct the same evaluation on the subject executive. The results typically showed significant levels of dissonance between the subject executives' view of themselves and the profiles provided by their associates.

To solve this problem, careful self-assessment, aided by various studies such as the Meyers-Briggs or Birkman Personality Assessment, are known to provide valuable information regarding an executive's key behavior, interests, professional and personal needs, and possible stress behaviors.

Probably the most accurate measure of the value of scientific and careful assessment is seen in the comment made to me by numerous clients upon discussing the results of these assessments:

I wish I had known these things about myself years ago. It would have helped me better manage communications and relationships on both personal and professional levels over the years.
— Ed, a 56-year-old engineering client

To be truly successful, you must know what works for you and what does not, who you succeed with and who you do not, what pace of business is best for you, what level of detail or open planning attracts and excites you, what amount of travel or lack thereof is ideal for you, etc. You should even be sensitive to how long a commute you can sustain. These are the human issues that we so often forget, or never knew in the first place about ourselves.

Every successful career search begins with deciding who you are and what you want to accomplish. You need to find the right job for you, with the right pay and benefits, at the right company, in the right field of business, with the right people. FOR YOU!

As mentioned in the previous chapter, I have created a **three-part Personal and Career Assessment Phase** that is designed to provide you with a clear sense of who you are, what you wish to do, and what you bring to the party, what is working for you and what are your primary barriers to gaining career success.

Assessment Phase — Part I

This first part is the Personal Mission Statement. Sit down with a cup of tea or glass of wine when things are quiet and you can focus on yourself. There are no "right" answers to this questionnaire. It is meant to elicit thoughts and reactions that will cause you to consider aspects of yourself, your career and your life, that you may have ignored or forgotten in the rush of daily life. Ideally, use a computer to record your answers so you can go back and edit later.

The **Personal Mission Statement** looks like this:

> **Brief Biography:** (your family, background, formal education highlights, sports, military, other observations — write about yourself at length)

> **My Focus of Value:** What ideas, beliefs, concepts, practices and goals do I hold most dear? (Example: I am a strong family person, place importance on my family, job, faith and friends; I am kind, considerate, supportive, intelligent, interested and ap-

proachable. I am patient with people, optimistic and energetic, etc.)

Personal and Career High/Achievements:

Personal and Career Disappointment:

What Does Success Look Like To Me:

Met Goals:

Un-met Goals:

Need Factors: What are my fears and concerns, and what three-four things are distracting me or not done:

Power Factors: Resources and tools I am equipped with now:

People (types) I work best with (specific names not required; general description is fine):

People (types) I work worst with:

References/Supporters:

Three companies I admire and why:

Three people I admire and why:

Any other thoughts and comments:

My favorite story is of a young, 28-year-old man, Matt, who had not graduated from college. He worked as a rock mason. He expressed a lack of confidence in his future and could not determine any sort of career path to pursue. We completed the assessment phase and found that he had strong interest in working with his hands (obviously), but in a very detailed and precise fashion.

> *He also volunteered that he admired his grandfather's clock collection and enjoyed taking some of the less-valuable models apart. I showed him the first four pages of the Wall Street Journal, which contained numerous ads for expensive watches. We agreed that those watches needed expert servicing at very high fees on an annual basis. Seeing the light at the end of the tunnel, Matt interviewed professional watch repairmen in San Francisco who told him there was a dearth of young talent in the profession. Finding a Rolex Watch-Making School in several cities, he applied and qualified for a scholarship, attended the two-year program, got married and returned to the Bay Area as a successful and very happy watch repair professional. He "owns" that role, come hell or high water. It is his brand, and he strongly believes in it.*

Assessment Phase — Part II

The second part of the Assessment Phase is the **Birkman Method** assessment (birkman.com). Many coaches rely on Myers-Briggs, Strong, and other systems, but my experience suggests that the Birkman Method provides much more information and guidance for ensuring your career is well-directed.

With the Birkman Method results, you will better understand yourself, how you "show up" in group environments, your professional strengths and weaknesses, your ideal job profile, your key needs and stress zones and the behavior you may adopt when under such stress.

You will learn about your true interests, jobs that people like you enjoy, important "needs" you have on the job and in your life, and insights into your stress behavior and how to avoid it.

The Birkman Method has been used by hundreds of companies throughout the world for over forty years with employees of all levels and professions. It also provides information on how you (and others) negotiate and sell, which are two very different subjects. You will learn the key requirements for both negotiations and sales processes, and how to identify and avoid stressful experiences in both negotiations with others and in sales activities.

Janet was frustrated in her position at a major university in the Alumni Relations Department. She was extremely effective at her position, but her Assessment Phase identified a significant distaste for administration (even though she did it well) and a strong desire to be part of something more innovative and creative. Within weeks of digesting this new learning from the Birkman Personality Test, she had contacted friends at another university and was hired in their marketing department to create new programs to expand alumni participation in various activities.

Most importantly, you will be provided action steps to manage improvement and change in your everyday life and professional activities. Your family, associates, friends and, most importantly, you, will see exciting results when you take the time to learn more about yourself and put that learning into action.

People from many professions and stages of life have greatly benefited from insights gained from the Birkman Method Professional Profile study.

Should you wish to take the Birkman Method process yourself, simply go to www.birkman.com, and follow the "Experience Birkman Yourself" prompts.

Should you wish to engage my coaching and interpretation of the Birkman Method, you can contact me to arrange a test date and debriefing with one-week turn-around timing.

Full Disclosure: I am a certified Birkman Method coach having conducted over 200 interpretations of the Birkman report and guided executives on how best to integrate the results of this study into their Career Action Plan.

A young graduate from a prestigious university, Hal, began working with me because he had little sense of what lay ahead for him. Shy and self-effacing, he took a dim view of his prospects. We began, as always, with the Assessment Phase during which he confirmed his "supportive nature" vs. having a "leadership nature." He also recognized his deep need to organize and "prove" the value of his work. Law emerged as one of his possible directions; he decided to take the Law Boards, was accepted and graduated from a leading law school a year ago. Knowing his profile, he pursued positions that were research-oriented vs. ones requiring a strong personal presentation focus. Succeeding in his search, he is happily working to help law partners prepare, analyze and win legal cases in the employment law field. He is filling the right role for himself, not someone else's idea (father's, uncle's, friends' idea) of what he should be doing.

Assessment Phase – Part III

The third part of the Assessment Phase is the "Crossing Your Rubicon" exercise.

This is an opportunity for you to identify the bridges and barriers to career success: what is working for you and what is working against your success.

Julius Caesar knew how to "take" Rome, but he must have had deep concerns regarding how to get his Army across the Rubicon River, which was a raging torrent in those days. So, he had to take stock of his army's ability to forge such a river before they could take on the battle of Rome.

Like Caesar, you have to consider the strengths and weaknesses, the "bridges" and "barriers" in your life, personal and professional, and gauge your overall preparedness to "attack Rome," or in your case, move boldly forward with your Action Plan.

For the Crossing the Rubicon exercise, sit down one evening and write brief responses to how prepared/supported your "army" feels in these areas:

1. Family (immediate and extended)

2. Health

3. Spiritual Life

4. Education

5. Technology

6. Personal Relationships

7. Intellectual Pursuits

8. Finances/Investments

9. Geographic satisfaction (Do you like where you live?)

10. Recreation and Fun

11. Office, Equipment, Memberships, Professional tools

Please consider the "status" of each item and how it could be improved if you wanted it improved/changed.

This provides you with a chance to get everything on the table that may be distracting you or that you have not fully considered or solved before you move on to developing your **Action Plan**. It clearly identifies your strengths and weaknesses so that you can promote the former and rectify the latter.

With these exercises and the Birkman Method assessment results, you will have concrete and actionable information on which to begin to build your Action Plan as you proceed along your **Crystal Clear Career Path**.

CHAPTER 3

Phase Two:
Develop an Action Plan —
Create Your Tools

You need a plan to build a house.
To build a life, it's even more important to have a plan.
— George Bernard Shaw

Now that you know yourself and your career goals more clearly, it is time to build your **Career Action Plan.**

The key pieces of this plan are as follows:

Your Communications Platform. This is the basis for ALL your communications. This document defines what is most valuable about you and what is said about you in your documents and conversations to prospective employers and networking contacts.

   Name/Date:

   Key Value Statement: (Succinct statement that captures your essence)

   Unique Points of Difference: (Statement of what is unique about you)

   Your Style: (How you do what you do)

Target Audience: (Who you want to reach)

Key Support Points: (What proves or supports your value statement)

Three to Four Support Stories: (Select some memorable stories as illustrations about your past work life. These should be impressive and include quantifiable results. Each story should illustrate a key aspect of your candidacy.)

Here is an example of a client's **Communications Platform:**

Key Value Statement: Twenty-year technology leader in the video graphics industry with special ability to build highly productive interdisciplinary teams, develop successful new consumer products on budget and under challenging time constraints, and support marketing/sales efforts via extensive public speaking activities.

Unique Points of Difference: The combination of my strong technology education (MBA) and extensive leadership experience, coupled with my ability to advocate and lead new product marketing efforts makes me uniquely qualified to play key roles in the development, refinement and marketing of leading-edge high tech products and services.

Your Style: I am a strong people-focused executive, able to attract and inspire smart people to achieve our agreed-upon goals. I am also very active, enjoy being among my people and customers, enjoy a positive and successful environment and making good things happen.

Target Audience: Technology leaders at mid-sized and large video/graphics-centric companies; CEO's of emerging video technology companies, and venture capital partners. Also targeting university technology thought-leaders.

Key Support Points:

- Masters, Electrical Engineering, USC; MBA Stanford University, numerous advanced study courses, professional association courses

- Twenty-year video technology leadership career at Sony, LSI Logic and AMD. Recognized subject expert, team-builder, and cost-sensitive product developer. Numerous hires have succeeded in important industry roles.

- Lead development of early video graphics cards and recent breakthroughs in video technology products associated with flat screen television

Stories: This executive's specific stories have been omitted for confidentiality. However, see below for two stories of how establishing a solid communications platform worked for two of my clients.

As you may have noticed, this is a simple but powerful document that crystallizes what this executive will say to people about himself. It ensures message clarity, consistency and accuracy while also being easy to memorize for use in answering that famous interview question, "Tell me about yourself."

Ned is thirty and recently married. He worked abroad for the past eight years following college, and is now trying to gain employment in the San Francisco Bay Area in the construction business. Fortunately, there are many jobs due to the tech explosion in the City. Unfortunately, Jake is a little perplexed as to how to identify and approach these companies as he feels out of touch, and perhaps under-qualified, for the right positions. Our work is primarily focused on creating a very concise and persuasive "story" for him to employ in written and verbal outreaches. Done properly, this will distinguish him from his competition and gain him an exciting and rewarding career back on his home turf.

Once your **Communications Platform** is developed, use that strategic document as the basis for creating these key tools:

Your resumé and your bio: Develop them for use in conversations, emails, job applications, etc. As there are numerous resources for helping you create your resumé and bio, I have chosen not to discuss them in detail in this book. Your resumé is your fact sheet; your bio is your story. Both are important.

Suffice it to say that your resumé should be no longer than two-pages, contain all your contact information, a focus statement that reflects your Key Value Statement at the top, provide your work and educational history in reverse chronological order with accurate dates, provide a brief personal statement. Do not offer to provide references (this is assumed and a waste of space). PROOF IT and email it to several people to ensure it transmits properly. Give the file a simple title: JohnSmith.resumé.

For good examples of bios, go to the websites of companies you respect and use the same format for your bio that you see for their key executives. Remember, it is your story; be sure to tell it well. Include your picture (semi-formal- shirt/no tie, collar blouse).

Your 60-Second Elevator Speech: Use this in conversations with people *who can help you* (That means almost everyone you run into).

Business Cards: Include your name, description of your professional focus (e.g., new food products marketing expert), cell phone (no home phone), email, LinkedIn address, home city, state.

Your Interviewing Skills: More on this later.

Your Email & Voicemail Templates: Include these three parts in both: (a) Why I am writing/calling to you, (b) Why I may "fit" your company and (c) I will call next week to arrange a meeting.

Here's an example of a good voicemail message:

"Hi, this is Frank Smith. I am calling because I saw on your very informative website that you are establishing a new division in natural food products.

My background at XYZ Company and ABC Company included extensive work in this area. My team achieved a xxx result with x% business growth in two years.

I would like to meet with you or one of your team members to learn how I might be able to help you achieve your business goals.

I will call at 10 AM next Tuesday in the hopes of having a phone call or setting a meeting. In the interim, should you wish to contact me, I can be reached at 444-333-2222 or at FrankSmith@...com.

Thanks very much."

A technology sales executive, Anne found the assessment phase very illuminating, causing her to recognize that what she had really been doing all along was "advocating" rather than simply selling computer-related products. Using the Communications Platform to guide her thinking, she re-cast her approach taking a more sophisticated positioning for herself as a "company spokesperson." She became energized around a new role for herself and changed her career goals to reflect this new and exciting insight. While she is still in the search phase, she is optimistic and excited about representing a company's mission to their primary audiences of consumers, investors and industry peers. (Note: Anne recently landed the job she had been seeking that lined up with her professional goals as well as enabling her to commute from her home city. The latter was important as she has small children).

Re-Activate Your Network. Make a list of everyone you have ever worked with. Begin to contact them to make them aware of your search and to ask for their help. Consider starting a weekly group of like individuals to meet and help each other with their career goals. Pay attention to contacting people who "sold to you" in prior jobs; they want your help in reaching others like you in your industry.

Re-Build Your Reference List. Include three supervisors, three peers and three subordinates. Ask their permission, update them on your search goals, and remind them of your strengths to refresh their memories. Keep them periodically updated on your progress. Alert them to calls from companies; ask them for feedback from reference calls. Treat them seriously and considerately. Use them only when it appears that the interview process is going very well.

Get Onto Three to Five Job Boards and Check In Weekly. Check indeed.com and simplyhire.com, netshare.com. Join sites like Lead411.com to stay abreast of industry activities that could help you.

Join LinkedIn and Create a Complete Home Page There. Include your bio, connections, recommendations, groups, and other items that LinkedIn will help you complete. Use the site aggressively to find people and companies in your industry. Be careful with popular social media sites like Facebook. Keep it very low key and professional. Do not invite inappropriate "friends."

Employers have become very adept at scouring the Internet to gain all types of information on applicants. Manage your social media accordingly.

For an in-depth understanding of how to get the most from LinkedIn, I asked Ted Prodromou, award-winning author of *Ultimate Guide to LinkedIn for Business* and *Ultimate Guide to Twitter for Business*, to be a guest author on the subject of getting the most from LinkedIn.

7 Steps to LinkedIn Success

By Ted Prodromou

LinkedIn is the largest professional network and the fastest growing social network. Currently LinkedIn is adding two new members every second and is growing faster than Facebook, Twitter and Google+ combined.

Despite it's rapid growth and popularity, most LinkedIn members haven't discovered its true power. Many still believe LinkedIn is a place to post your resumé and look for jobs. Those who understand the power of LinkedIn are gaining a huge competitive advantage.

Here are seven tips that will help you get started with LinkedIn.

1. **Create a LinkedIn strategy:** To get the most from LinkedIn, you need to have a clear strategy with trackable goals. Your LinkedIn strategy should be an integral part of your social media strategy. Every post should be done for a specific reason like offering a whitepaper, promoting an event, or providing valuable information to your followers.

2. **Complete your profile:** Most LinkedIn members don't complete their profile, which can project an unprofessional image. Imagine if your website was only 50% complete. Once you complete your LinkedIn profile, you start appearing in LinkedIn search results more often and your viewers know exactly how you can help them.

3. **Post status updates and publish content regularly:** The more information you share, the more people will view your profile and connect with you. Sharing valuable information on a regular basis establishes you as a expert in your niche.

4. **Grow your network:** Add at least two people to your network every day. It only takes a few seconds to send a personalized invitation. Every time you see an interesting LinkedIn profile in your sidebar or in the newsfeed, reach out to them and ask them how you can help them.

5. **Participate in Groups:** Find three to five active groups where your target audience hangs out and join those groups. Participate in conversations by

sharing valuable information. Focus on helping others and never self-promote. If you do promote yourself heavily, you can be flagged as a spammer.

6. **Start a Company page:** A LinkedIn Company page is a mini-website for your company. You can post content, post job openings and promote offers to your customers. LinkedIn is currently enhancing the company page templates giving your company more exposure to LinkedIn's 300 million members. LinkedIn Company pages also appear in Google search results, which is an added benefit.

7. **Be consistent:** Like everything in life, consistency is the key to success. The more active you are on LinkedIn, the more people will connect with you, which expands your customer base. The bigger your customer base is, the more money you earn.

Do a little bit each day and you will see success. People see your name every day and they get to know, like and trust you because you are always there sharing great information and helping others.

For more information, visit tedprodromou.com or email Ted at info@tedprodromou.com.

CHAPTER 4

Phase Three: Execute Your Action Plan Every Day

To be, or not to be: that is the question.
— Shakespeare, *Hamlet*

C learly, the most important step you must take is one of action. It is good to do all the work that we have discussed, but unless you put it into action on a daily basis, it will have no value.

Given that you have to "be" your search constantly, here are the "Must Do's" of your search, the steps you should take to implement your **Action Plan**:

Create your Key Target Company List: Your goal is a list of **ten to twenty companies** where you want to work and where you deserve to work.

✓ **Identify companies within thirty miles** or so of your home (for a reasonable commute).

✓ **Create a database** (use freecrm.com to keep organized with your companies and contacts).

✓ **Learn all you can from their websites** and by Googling the company.

✓ **Identify management and board members** with whom you have an affinity (e.g. college, business focus, sports, etc.)

✓ **Contact one to three of these people per company** via phone AND email. Use the three-part email (why I'm contacting you, why I "fit" with your firm's business, I will call next week to set a meeting.)

✓ **Begin to build relationships** and keep them forever in your Active Network.

✓ **Find out what Companies are focused on right now** via their "Press Release" section of their website. Go to conferences that they are attending, contact current execs, check LinkedIn past executives with whom to network.

✓ **Learn the keys to Effective/Winning telephone interviews.** 90% of your job search will be via the phone. **See Chapters 7 and 8** for the little-known techniques to ensure that your phone interview gets you to the next step — the live interview.

✓ **Join a professional networking site** like MENG (Marketing Executives Network Group- mengonline.com) FENG, and others where you can view job postings, ask if people know people at certain companies, etc. Get familiar with how to get the most out of these websites- smart people do!

✓ **Get a buddy or several friends who are also seeking work** and form an *accountability group* to ensure someone else is helping you stay on your mission, every day. Help them do the same.

✓ **Contact headhunters.** The key is to "help" them as well as ask them for help. Suggest that you can provide leads etc. on active searches in your area of specialization. They'll be surprised by your offer, and likely more available to you.

✓ **Contact target company executives and other potential sources of hiring including** *board members.* As discussed in a later chapter, you should have a list of 10-20 companies within 30 miles (decent commute) of your home and learn all about them via the Press Release section, bios and board member profiles. Target board members as they have time to meet, and possibly, are frustrated with the executives in the area in which you have interest.

✓ **Begin to arrange informational interviews** with people you identify who are somehow linked to your Target Companies. Try to arrange coffee or lunch dates. Be sure to think about how to best leverage the meeting and be sure to follow-up with a thank-you note and let them know later on how they helped make a difference for you when you land.

✓ **Always send thank you notes, preferably in writing/snail mail.** Note one or two key items you discussed and restate your sincere interest and reasons for joining the company. Put their names on a follow-up list for monthly contacts, even if nothing takes place near-term.

Do these things on a weekly basis. Do not lose heart or focus. This is not easy work, but the results are awesome.

CHAPTER 5

Ten Steps to Getting Work that Works for You

Winning is not a sometime thing; it's an all time thing.
Winning is habit. Unfortunately, so is losing.
— Vince Lombardi

Here is the "short list" for a career search:

1. **Learn** who you really are and want via testing, coaching, networking

2. **Express** your Key Selling Statement, Unique Point-of-Difference and your Key Support Points in a Candidate Communications Document.

3. **Identify** your key target audience: who most needs to know about your candidacy and who needs you. Create a strong, vibrant bio and resumé.

4. **Build and communicate** with a robust networking group. Use LinkedIn to do this as well as other methods to reach out to people you know to help.

5. **Identify ten to twenty companies** located where you currently or wish to live that you want to work at and where you "deserve" (are qualified) to work.

6. **Aggressively research** the companies; locate executives (management, board members, VC's, mid-level managers via LinkedIn) with whom you have some synergy and who could help you navigate to a job opportunity.

7. **Decide** that you are seeking "work that works for you," not just another job. Define that work (content, reporting relationship, staff, project process, etc.) to the point where you will know the right opportunity for you when you see it.

8. **Call/email** with a brief three-point brief message (why I like your company, why I "fit," I will call in three days to set a meeting) that builds interest in you, and improves the chances for an initial meeting. Get that first meeting. At the very least, they will become part of your growing network.

9. **Follow-up bi-weekly**, be forceful and confident. Revise/refine the company list and people targets as you go along. Schedule specific time each week for this outreach.

10. **Go back to #1** and start over again the first of every month. Don't let up. Have fun at this, go for the goal, move down the field and be proactive.

CHAPTER 6

Should You Have Your Own Business?

Look for rewarding work, not just a job.
— Peter G. Engler, *Your Crystal Clear Career Path*

L et's take a breath here and consider that question. My bias is yes! Why? Because, sooner or later you will be self-employed, so why not do it earlier, rather than later?

This may sound like a flip response, but the world is trending towards entrepreneurship and individual business ownership.

Why?

1. Companies are hiring outside consultants on a need-to-have basis, rather than staffing like they used to do.

2. They are hiring experts in specific areas rather than generalists.

3. They have found that it is more cost-effective and productive.

4. Individual consultants have learned that the revenue can be very attractive and the oppor-

tunity to control their time and talent outweighs the benefits of a traditional job.

Do keep in mind that you can make this decision at any time as you travel down your Crystal Clear Career Path. Everything covered in this book can be applied whether you go for being hired as an employee or as a consultant. Here is the story of one of my clients that clearly illustrates this point.

> *Kevin contacted me two years ago to engage my services. He had lost his twenty plus year position at a major conglomerate in spite of his having led their successful move into new markets. He initially was focused on obtaining a CEO position in his field, a direction that I felt might not be very productive given the limited number of companies in that industry. However, we worked to build his candidacy and he had three promising options in which he was "runner-up." Reading the "tea leaves," Kevin began to adopt the backup strategy that we had identified of consulting in his field. He was going to market his valuable set of knowledge, his "expertise," on his own behalf. Within four months, he had three excellent clients, was working on projects that excited and rewarded him, and had the flexibility of having his own business at the age of 58. Instead of facing unemployment again at some point, he was fully self-employed, and more than pleased with his new "expert" role with his clients.*

CHAPTER 7

The Art of the Interview

You must be the change you wish to see in the world.
— Mahatma Gandhi

The interview is the most feared and misunderstood aspect of a career or job search. It is seen by both the candidate as well as the interviewing personnel as an uncomfortable and difficult event.

It should not have to be that.

It is actually one more event in human relations: sort of like a first date, a meeting with a new professor or a chance meeting with someone in a coffee shop.

It is simply an opportunity to check out your chemistry with someone else.

The interviewer(s) already have your resumé. They know what you are likely to be capable of doing on the job in question.

What they really want to know is: "How is this person going to work, act and succeed with us on this particular assignment and beyond?"

Nothing more, nothing less. A chemistry check.

Their objective in an interview: To enable the recruiter to assess your management and leadership chemistry, your core competencies and skills, your accomplishments and achievements (with metrics), and your potential to transfer those results to the position in question. More importantly they also want to ensure there is a "fit" between you and the company and the specific team you will be working with. This latter objective — checking the "chemistry" — is generally of primary importance to the interviewer.

Your objective in an interview: Have a conversation instead of an interview. You are a mature, experienced executive now, so it should not be the same as an interview was like when you were 25 or 30 years old. Turn it into a conversation between two people interested in the same thing.

You want them to like you and sense that you are a ready fit with their company's culture and business plans. You want to make it an easy, low risk event to hire you.

There are two main kinds of interviews: on the phone and in person. What follows are some powerful tips for you to implement for each type. There are certainly things that pertain to both, given that both types are basically conversations. Just the medium is different.

Tips for the Phone Interview

These tips have been gleaned from Human Resources Managers, hiring executives, outplacement company coaches and my own experience. They are crucial to conducting what may seem like an innocuous phone interview. However, the phone interview is really the gateway to obtaining a live interview with a company.

Before the call, review your company research and the job description. Have your resumé, bio, LinkedIn page and other personal documents at hand. Be prepared to take notes. Know all you can about the job, the company and your match with the opportunity.

Thoroughly think through the job requirements and write down bullet points that clearly qualify you for the job.

Be at your phone on time. Dress for the call. It is best to have arranged that you would call at a specific time so that you can have at least a modicum of control over the call. If they are calling you, answer the phone on the third ring with a pleasant ("Hello, this is [your name]") with a slightly formal tone. Have a glass of water at hand and perhaps, have taken some honey or a lozenge to smooth your voice. Also, remember to "wake up" your voice before the call if it is early in the morning.

Conduct the call from home or a quiet place. A landline is best, as you may have a bad cell connection and not realize it. Ensure that no family members or associates are liable to interrupt your call. Put the dog outside and turn off the TV.

Stand up and smile during the interview. Put up a picture (of them if possible) and speak to it. You will sound more energetic and powerful, and will likely be more focused regarding your comments.

Avoid letting the call lose energy, which is more likely to happen than with a live interview. Keep your responses and comments focused, brief, energetic and informative. Smile into the phone; chuckle a few times. Be "human" — all they know of you is your voice and your resumé. Remember that a phone interview may be conducted by a junior Human Resources employee, and therefore, they may not be an effective interviewer. Help the process along as best you can.

Enjoy yourself. This is a very preliminary — *but important* — interview, and perhaps in an odd interviewing environment, so simply be present and go for it. You will do fine if you prepare and think about your answers before speaking!

Refer to "Tips for the In-Person Interview" below for other suggestions.

Tips for the In-Person Interview

These are things to consider while preparing for a live interview:

Be half an hour early to the facility. Bring a notebook. Go immediately to the restroom and check your appearance carefully. Especially check your hair and teeth for neatness and evidence of breakfast or lunch. Check in with reception or the admin fifteen minutes early.

Expect to wait ten or more minutes. Be extremely cordial and pleasant with the receptionist and other "admin" folks. They are often asked later about their impressions of you. Bring a *Wall Street Journal* or industry publication with you and be reading it when they come for you. Greet them with a smile and a hello, and treat them like one of the interviewers. In fact, they may be an important member of the interviewing team. Remember to smile pleasantly. They will remember that first impression later when the boss asks what they thought of you. This process will also help you relax.

Take a few deep breaths as you proceed to the meeting room. **Remember to think of this as a meeting, one of hundreds you have had**. All you have to do is find common ground and proceed from there. You are there to help them solve a problem: "Who are we going to hire for this key position?" If asked, accept only some water. Coffee and other refreshments are distracting to the interview process.

Upon entering the office or meeting room, place your briefcase (which should be of good quality and not scuffed or "used" looking) against the wall, not on the table or desk. Pull out your leather notebook and a good-quality ballpoint pen, and place them on the table, perhaps adding your business card (very simple; just your name and contact information, no descriptor).

Remain standing, perhaps looking out the window. This is not the time to read anything. It *is* the time to take another breath, if you are alone, and to gather yourself. Smile again to yourself. Think that this is going to be a great meeting.

When they arrive, greet them much as you would anyone in any meeting you have had in the past. Be deferential, but not too deferential. **Remember, you are a pro and you are there because they need you to help them.**

Take your seat at the same time as they do. Be sure not to sit at the head of the table. Do not open your notebook right away; do it a bit into the interview when something interesting has come up and ask if they mind if you take some notes. They are likely to be impressed as you are "honoring" them and the meeting.

Have a copy of your resumé available, but not in clear sight. Have already titled your notes with their name, title, date and time. Do not note the company (it would appear that they are one of many interviews today, which is not the right message). Ease your business card across to them. It is then that they will pull out your resumé or realize they forgot to bring it. This is a great time to pull your copy out of your portfolio.

Take notes periodically and ask the interviewer for clarification of a question or for information at certain points in the meeting. This gives the interview the feeling of a conversation rather than a static series of questions and answers.

Remember, you are a professional. Speak with confidence and in fact, some passion. Be present in the meeting with good eye contact. Vary your posture from relaxed (not slouching), to relative intensity and back to relaxed. Avoid touching your face or smoothing your hair, wringing your hands or other unconscious gestures that portray anxiety, nervousness, or even, evasiveness.

Let them take control of the meeting. However, stay present and responsive. Don't interrupt or speak to fast. Keep your poise and keep things mostly relaxed.

Be prepared for these key questions:

1. "Tell me about yourself" — This is the big one, and the one that often derails the conversation. Have your "story" well-rehearsed and limit your answer to three or four minutes. Let them ask you to expand on certain points. Those are the issues they really want to explore with you.

2. "Why are you interested in (or qualified for) this position?"

3. "What would you do in your first ninety days here?"

4. "What would your peers / subordinates / managers say about you?"

5. "What are your most memorable accomplishments?"

6. "What are failures from which you have learned/recovered?"

Avoid dominating or taking over the interview!! (Especially if you are male and over 45.) The main thing they are trying to evaluate is the chemistry: yours with theirs. **Cool your jets** and avoid pressing any aspect of the conversation too aggressively. Avoid long-winded responses, war-stories and other self-oriented comments. Do not flatter them or comment directly about them ("Love your dress" and "Like your tie" do not belong in an interview. Make it easy for them to like you and make it low-risk for them to hire you.

Your goal is to adroitly shift the interview into a meeting. Said another way, you want to initiate some information sharing, and then reach some mutually attractive observations and agreements.

While it is *their* **meeting,** take opportunities to steer the meeting into areas of your strengths. If they ask you about your team-building expertise, provide three examples of achievements in this area and then expand on one of them in which you generated particularly distinctive results. This "three-point" structure helps you communicate important information in a concise and memorable manner.

Sit comfortably alert and interested, not back in your chair. When it becomes very evident that they love you, perhaps then you can sit back in your chair — in relief!

Answer the questions directly and briefly. If you are not sure of the question, ask for clarification. If you do not like your answer, ask if you fully responded to their question. You may get a second chance. Otherwise, forget it and move on. You have rehearsed the answers to numerous questions, so simply answer them, directly and briefly.

✓ Keep your answers **on point and brief**. Use examples, metrics, results, brief anecdotes (do not tell any lengthy stories — you will bore both of you) and third-party evaluations. Do not speak too long. Ask if you have been responsive to the question or do they want you to expand on any points. If you are over forty, do not over-sell yourself; be a pro, an expert and keep the energy moderate (interested but not heated with self-promotion). Keep it a little light and fun if possible. Make them want you because they trust you to work within their corporate style and culture. Being "overqualified" often means you scared them.

✓ Keep it all about **successful events and activities**. Avoid spending too much time on weaknesses in your resumé, past problems, negative interpersonal issues and other factors that do not present you in a positive fashion. Be honest and forthcoming about any such issues, but endeavor to move on. *Never belittle your current or past jobs, companies or associates.*

Smile, shift your body periodically, lean forward when something captures your passion, ease back to give some breathing room to the interviewer at various points. Do not touch your face, wring your hands, flip your pen or adjust your tie or clothing. Sit at ease with your hands in your lap. Remember to breath and smile pleasantly.

Take opportunities to ask a few questions, but not too many. It is their meeting. These questions should be focused on the job and the company, not on the interviewer (you really do not care about their golf game or kids at this point). Probe for information on why the job is open, previous incumbent, division history and current objectives, and the top four or five objectives for the next six or twelve months. You might also find a way to learn more about their own experience at the company, and what the interviewer feels has gone well and what needs additional attention.

Provide **brief recaps of or acknowledge receiving key information**. This, like taking a few notes, communicates that you are interested, are listening and value the information. It also compliments the other party in a professional fashion.

Seek opportunities to summarize your comments, again briefly and cogently; (e.g. "So, in response to your interest in my most significant team-building achievements, I was able to dramatically upgrade our campus recruiting program, reduce training expenses by 30-40%, and completely reorganize our national sales support team while reducing expenses by over twenty percent."

It will be evident when they wish to complete the interview. Look for such signs and stop talking. If they want to continue, they will say so.

At the conclusion, ask them how they felt it went and what they saw as next steps. This will elicit a favorable or unfavorable response. This is useful, as you want to know as soon as possible whether you should expend more energy on this opportunity. Getting an early "read" helps in this effort. Continue to be confident — it is only when they say "no" that you have to go into "damage control." (See below).

Thank them for their interest in you (not for "taking the time to meet you." — empty words). This will remind them that they should be interested in you, and will keep the momentum moving forward on your candidacy.

Do not provide references at the interview. Suggest that your references are busy people, and you would prefer to provide them at a later point in the process. They should appreciate this point of view; if they do not, you have one clear reason for not proceeding. You should also know that they will conduct an offline reference check among their own contacts.

Gather your belongings with reasonable alacrity and make your exit. Avoid stopping to chat with anyone, even old friends who may be present. A brief hello and "let's get together" should suffice without appearing churlish. The point here is to be business-like and professional. The high-fives will come later.

Feel free to **ask if they have key questions or concerns**. You can even ask, "how it went" in their minds, and what are the next steps.

If possible, **summarize the three key reasons you are interested in** and qualified for the opportunity and elicit, if possible, their agreement. These are the key elements you want to "stick" in the head(s) of the interviewer.

Be sure you have **their contact information for a follow-up thank-you note,** which should be sent by the next day. In the note, briefly recap your interest, the three or four reasons you feel the job is right for you and offer to provide any additional information they may require to keep the dialogue active. This can be sent via email (put your name in the subject line to quell spam).

Send a separate handwritten note to everyone with whom you met via snail mail. A separate, hand-written note is one of those "old-fashioned" tactics that still work in your favor. They still make a good impression today — sometimes an even better impression than the ubiquitous email.

Immediately follow-up with your recruiter or any-one who has "sponsored" you to keep them abreast of how you feel the meeting went. Discuss any ap-propriate next steps with them and elicit specific action steps on their part.

And lastly, remember there is no perfect interview-ing guidance — just ideas that seem to prove true, year after year.

Damage Control — If Needed

In certain cases, you will feel that the interview is not go-ing well, or after the fact, that you were not at your best. Here is what to do if you feel the meeting (or even the phone interview) is not going well, or afterwards you real-ize that it could have gone better:

State your concern and take responsibility. Suggest that you feel that he/she is not obtaining what they are seek-ing in the meeting, and ask them to clarify or provide more background to their questions. He/she may not be a good interviewer and their weakness could translate into an uncomfortable and unproductive meeting if you do not take control and get it back on track.

Do so with patience, grace and even good humor. Re-member, you are likely to be older and more experienced than the initial interviewer (be they a recruiter or compa-ny executive), so they may be somewhat intimidated by you and the process.

Tell your **recruiter or "sponsor" immediately following the interview** that you suspect that it did go well/not well in your opinion. The sooner they know, the sooner they can check in with the interviewer to corroborate your assessment. If there has been a problem, ask them to help get the process back on track. This is a key time to "use" your recruiter or sponsor or any other people on your behalf.

Decide if the failure of a portion of or all of the interview suggests that the job is simply wrong for you. The interview should be a guide to your thought process regarding your level of interest in the opportunity. If they cannot staff an interview effectively, you should be concerned regarding in what other areas they are insufficiently staffed.

In general, you will be successful in interview evolutions for jobs or consulting opportunities that are "right" for you and, frankly, unsuccessful in interviews for opportunities that are not "right."

You and the other party will know within the first few minutes of the interview if there are green or red lights flashing. This chemistry check is the most significant aspect of any interviewing situation (or, for that fact, any meeting), and will play the largest role in the eventual outcome. Be aware of your instincts as you proceed with the interview, and if they continue to be negative, suggest that you and the interviewer terminate the meeting in a gracious manner. You will be doing both of you a favor. It is also possible that the company will contact you to determine what occurred. This could lead to another (and more productive) meeting with a more qualified interviewer.

In any event, keep track of how each interview went and enter notes to guide you in future interviews. "Grade" yourself on key factors such as presence, brevity, ability to answer the questions, and a general overall score on interviewing performance.

In closing, it is a good idea to practice; have "dry runs" with friends or executives who are highly experienced in the art of the interview. Career coaches practice in most major cities, and are great sources of candid and experienced interviewing advice and coaching.

A fifty-year old woman with a strong technology marketing background, Alicia, wanted to pursue her long-time interest in joining a major non-profit in the Washington, D.C. area. She enjoyed the assessment phase, especially some of the learning around her "true needs" in a job, and carefully evaluated over ten corporate and non-corporate non-profit entities. Patiently pursuing senior executives at those organizations that she had identified as her "Top 10 Targets", she made strong connections via email and phone, which were followed by in-person meetings (not "interviews"). She clearly sought "work, not just a job." She made the interviewing process a key part of the search as a research tool. Recently, she began work as a General Manager of one of her top five non-profit target firms with a strong compensation package and an exciting mission to lead.

CHAPTER 8

Key Insights Into
Effective Interviewing

You have to learn the rules of the game. And then you have to play better than anyone else.
— Albert Einstein

On top of the detailed information provided in the previous chapter, here are some "big picture" things for you to take in and apply as you go through the interview process.

1. Always present a "helping attitude."

2. Talk less, listen more. "Cool your jets" a bit. Find out what they really need.

3. Smile, even when you are not happy. Smile. Smile.

4. Dress a click above the environment. This shows respect and people like that.

5. Build and keep your Network active and healthy.

6. Build and cherish your References. Provide them only when the job looks real.

7. Create and polish your resumé. Ensure your Bio tells an interesting story that makes people want to meet you. Avoid typos and incomplete information.

8. Avoid long, hellish commutes.

9. Do not "underprice" yourself and your services; your expertise is of real value.

10. Have confidence in yourself, your achievements, your age, and your objectives. If you do not, no one else will.

11. "Be the Ball." That reference to the movie *Caddyshack* means represent your passion in everything that you do.

12. Don't worry about what others think. Most of the time, they are thinking about themselves anyway.

13. In interviews, focus on what you think they need and try to solve it. Provide brief, thoughtful answers, relax, smile, have some pithy questions ready, smile, and "ask how it went and what is next."

14. Remember, you are interviewing for an offer, not a job, per se. Once you get the offer, you are now in the catbird seat and can endeavor to revise the job more to your needs while keeping their needs clearly in mind.

15. Act your age. Enjoy and value your age. Smile.

16. Always remember to *thank* everyone who helped you at critical points in your career.

Jack, a highly accomplished financial-services marketing executive, found himself out of options, or so he thought, after his company was acquired. He thought being fifty and somewhat "long-in-the-tooth" would work against him in his search. In our meetings, we focused on his areas of "expertise" that would be highly valued by prospective employers. We ignored his age (fortunately, he was in great shape) and simply promoted his wide-ranging marketing prowess. Finding a federal credit union close to his home, he was surprised to learn they were hiring for two positions that he could easily fill. The problem was that both paid about half of his salary objectives. I suggested he ask them to consider merging the two positions with a concurrent increase in salary (that actually saved the bank money) that was what he was seeking. He has been happily at work for almost two years at this point, and making major contributions to his new company.

CHAPTER 9

How to Keep the Job
Once You Have Landed It

Live as if you were to die tomorrow. Learn as if you were to live forever.
— Mahatma Gandhi

T he first six months are the most important months in a new job. This seems pretty obvious, but people often forget it in the heat of getting underway with their new responsibilities.

This critical activity is called "on-boarding." You have to ensure it happens well for you.

The surprising fact is that many companies do not carefully manage the new employee's transition into the company, and therefore miss an great opportunity to ensure his or her success, and in turn, their success.

Here are some suggestions to keep in mind the day you walk through those new front doors:

✓ Be sure to say hello to the receptionist, and nod or say hello to everyone else. Smile.

✓ Try to remember peoples' names; this is difficult, but people are impressed with individuals who make the effort to do so.

- ✓ Your boss(s) is/are your future; be sure you thoroughly understand them and their objectives.

- ✓ Note the company practices and style around punctuality, lots of conversation or very little conversation, details or broad strokes, numbers or ideas, early morning meetings or end-of-the-day meetings, etc. Try to understand and respond to their needs as appropriate.

- ✓ Understand *your* needs. If you are not able to work in a manner that you know suits you and generates your best work, then endeavor to shift your environment slowly but surely. If early morning meetings are not your cup of tea, start holding late afternoon meetings with your staff/peers to shift them into that mode. If lots of detail is not your strong suit, make friends with people who love details and ask them to support you in your activities.

- ✓ Smile and relax. People feel better around happy people.

- ✓ Join a company sports team or special work group. Find ways to quietly, yet productively do more than just your job.

- ✓ Find a mentor within the company, perhaps in a different group or division, who knows the company and is someone you admire. Become friends and begin to seek their advice. They will be flattered and will very likely play a key role in your successful growth in the company.

- ✓ Make friends with HR. They have a significant impact on your success.

✓ Make friends with board members. They care about the company, have "skin" in the game, and have a large impact on organizational issues.

✓ Do not complain, take sides, gossip, or express your negative reactions to events. Instead, be a vision of positive thinking and action. You will be appreciated for that — and rewarded.

When done right, this "on-boarding" process will smooth your way and help you achieve success and happiness in your new company.

Ideas to Help You Along Your Crystal Clear Career Path

The following chapters contain my thinking about various aspects of a career search. They are strictly my views and are offered for your consideration (and rejection should you so choose).

The point of each of them is that a career search is a highly personal and personalized mission. Each individual must shape their own search on the basis of their own self-assessment, action plan and action plan implementation.

It is really up to you, as we have said. A Proactive Search will be more exciting and more successful than the traditional mode of waiting for headhunters and old business associates to call with bright ideas.

Do the work. Relish the trip. Enjoy the results.

CHAPTER 10

Crossing Your Career Rubicon River

One of the most important aspects of getting a better job, changing careers, or if unemployed, finding a new position or consulting assignment, is to ensure that you are fully prepared in all aspects of your life to succeed in this important quest.

I call this process, "Crossing Your Career Rubicon River."

Julius Caesar was an experienced general and knew how to "take" Rome. But, he had deep concerns regarding getting his Army across the Rubicon River, which was a raging torrent in those days. So, he had to take stock of his army's abilities, unit by unit, to safely forge the river before he could wage the battle of Rome.

Like Caesar, we have to consider in our career planning and execution, the strengths and weaknesses, the "bridges" and "barriers" in our lives, personal and professional, and gauge our overall preparedness to "attack Rome," to move boldly with our Career Action Plan. As they say, success is found in the adroit execution of the plan, not just the plan.

So, find a time to write down how prepared your "Army" is in these critical areas:

Family (immediate and extended). Do you have a sick parent whose illness is distracting you? Is a wayward child distracting you from the career issues you want to solve? Is a wounded friendship causing you to lose sleep?

Health. Should you schedule that physical soon? Do you need to lose forty pounds of weight? You will look younger and have more energy for your search if you do.

Spiritual Life. Do you feel a gap in your spiritual life that you would like to satisfy? Have you learned about other types of Faith of which you have been curious?

Education. Should you finally earn that MBA, or attend some evening classes to sharpen your computer or writing skills?

Technology. Do you really know how to get the most out of your cell phone or tablet? Would a course in Power Point or Excel help you in your communications with others?

Personal Relationships. Do you have a close group of supporters? Do you have a "rabbi" to whom you can go for insights and guidance? Are your references an active resource of guidance and help to you?

Intellectual Pursuits. Are you reading or attending lectures regularly? Have you wanted to start doing crossword puzzles, but put it off?

Finances/Investments. How are your reserves? Have you sat down with a financial advisor to begin to update your investment strategies? Have you planned effectively for retirement?

Geographic satisfaction. Where you live? As you get older, it becomes more important to "be happy." Living where you want to live is a big part of personal happiness. Consider moving if you have another location in mind, or consciously dig into your current town and learn more about it.

Recreation and Fun. Exercise, walk, bike or whatever. Every day. You don't need an expensive trainer or gym. They say half an hour most days of the week will keep you in good shape. Would adopting a pet bring more joy and laughter into your life? Would special nights out with your spouse or friend bring a boost to your life?

Office / equipment / memberships / professional tools. Is it time to upgrade your laptop, to buy a tablet or to upgrade your backup system?

Please consider the "status" of each item and how it could be improved.

This provides you with a chance to get everything "on the table." Set action steps to address unresolved issues in each "army unit."

Once you have done this work, you can more confidently "Cross Your Rubicon" and more easily take the "Rome" of your career.

CHAPTER 11

Hemingway Was a Career Coach

I recently re-read Hemingway's brief (only 125 pages!) but remarkable novel, *The Old Man and the Sea*.

It is clear to me that not only was "Papa" a unique and powerful writer, he also knew a great deal about life and its many individual achievements and unexpected challenges. He would have made an excellent career coach.

With the time-honored privilege of editorial license afforded writers (and coaches, I hope), I have gleaned a number of themes from the novel that apply to effective career planning.

- ✓ A job search, like a fishing expedition, requires courage and faith. Santiago may have been old, but he was "cheerful and undefeated." It was this deep sense of optimism, even at his advanced age that caused him to think, "tomorrow is going to be a good day with this current."

- ✓ Age should not be allowed to temper our efforts and confidence in ourselves. "Many made fun of the old man and he was not angry."

- ✓ A job search is made easier and more successful if we learn to trust and rely on others. Santiago

did not initially act on the numerous offers of
help from the boy, Manolin, a hero-worshiping
youth from his village. As the novel progresses,
he accepts the small but meaningful assistance
of the boy with encouraging results.

✓ Set your career sights a little broader as does
Santiago when he ventures farther out to sea
than he has ever "fished" before.

✓ Take good care of yourself, stay in shape, and
learn new things. Santiago was in good physical
condition, maintained his boat and equipment,
and was an ardent baseball fan, something that
took his mind off his unproductive fishing business. Find passions for yourself like Santiago's
"the great DiMaggio."

✓ Replace your youthful ambition with mature
modesty and confidence as Santiago does when
the boy asserts that he is the best fisherman in
the village. "No, I know others [who are] better."

✓ Realize that your youthful energy may have
waned somewhat, and rely instead on your
"tricks and resolution" to make your objectives
and dreams come true. Focus on "the lions on
the beach" as Santiago does in his dreams, rather than on the negative events of the past.

✓ "Let the current take you out to where the big
fish are." The "current" consists of career aids
including LinkedIn, employment websites,
Hoover's, company websites, past associates
and other resources.

✓ Define your targets carefully, like Santiago did, based upon where you really want to work and where you belong, "and maybe there will be a big one among the bonito and the albacore." Find work, "a big one just made for you," not just a job, another small fish that will not challenge or feed you.

✓ Just as "Albacore make beautiful bait" for Santiago, ensure that your bait (resumé, bio, elevator speech, email and voice-mail script, target list, thoughtful interview questions, etc.) is fresh and guaranteed to get a big bite. Like Santiago, who considers the fish and their needs and lives, be sure you are considering the company, their people, and their possible challenges, and be responsive to those factors in your interviews.

✓ Once you have created interest in yourself and they "have taken the bait," let the company run with it as they will need a period of time to make a decision, but stay alert and close, checking in "with your fingers on the line" and anticipating various developments with thoughtful inquiries and responses.

✓ Continue to "re-bait your line with fresh thinking and ideas," see to your health, keep "an eye on the weather" and prepare for the coming of the sharks (unexpected events that might strip the opportunity from your fishing line). Don't give up. Santiago didn't!

✓ Be prepared to finally land the great fish by anticipating how to bring it alongside your boat and securely lash it. "Clear up [your] head, clear up" as you negotiate the new opportunity and ensure that it is the right job for you with the right incentives and support elements that will assure success and happiness.

✓ Realize that others may never fully appreciate your achievement. Santiago's fellow fishermen saw only a ravaged skeleton tied to his boat, "eighteen feet from nose to tail." Only the individual fishing for that giant of all fish (or job) can fully appreciate what it means to him or her to land it, and how much meat is really on those bones (and job). Like the Old Man gently asleep at the close of the novel, happily dreaming of lions on the beach, one can only contemplate and prepare for another day at sea.

Happy Fishing!!

CHAPTER 12

"Belief" — The Key to Stronger Personal Branding

I was speaking with an executive the other day regarding my career coaching practice and he asked me what I thought about developing "my Brand."

Like many of you, I have grown skeptical of lots of many of the career coaching buzz and noise around hot topics like how to use Twitter to market yourself (you need loads and months of tweets), the value of a personal website (you have that on LinkedIn, right?), tweaking your resumé for every job you pursue (HR "can smell" that, can't they?) and other current "hot" ideas.

I replied that understanding yourself in great detail through an intensive personal assessment process, translating that information into a strong and vibrant bio (your "story," which should be exciting and persuasive), 60-second elevator speech and other communications including your emails/voicemails, and directing it to people who can actually help you at companies where you "deserve to work" makes good sense.

If you want to call that "branding," great. It certainly has worked for many famous products, so why couldn't it work for job seekers?

However, what is missing from the "branding" idea is your beliefs; your energy, convictions, personality, motivations, desires, and all that makes you a special human being and professional.

I call this important duality of Branding (*who* you are) and Belief (*why* you are you), *Brand Belief*.

Your beliefs bring you alive to the reader, interviewer or person you have just met at a business mixer. Sure, you have to give people a sense of who you are and what you do — your Brand. However, it is the level of conviction and energy — your Belief — that you apply to that branding message that is what people will remember and act on.

You may be a terrific marketing executive, but until someone sees the fire in your eyes when you explain how you drill down to find every fact to support your new product concept, your Brand will just be another brand. Belief brings credibility to your Brand.

Credibility is what people buy, hire and remember. *Brand Belief* is what I believe you need to write down, refine and communicate to others, not just your Brand.

CHAPTER 13

Are We a Fit?

It is not surprising to realize that the primary purpose of a job interview, or even a casual conversation around a possible business association is, "are we a fit?" "Can we work successfully together?"

When you are in a 1:1 meeting to discuss your candidacy for an opportunity, you have already passed the test of having the right credentials and experience for the most part. They have reviewed your resumé and your terrific bio and know you *professionally* to a certain extent.

What they really want to know is the answer to the classic question, "tell me about yourself."

They want to know how you think, interact with people, size up and solve problems, deal with stress; how you are to work with. The interviewer (and the company) wants to know how successful you will be at the company. How you will "fit in."

This is especially true the older you are. Young people can be trained and molded to a company culture; older folks bring years of acculturation elsewhere to the party. This can prove problematic in many cases.

So what to do?

I believe that the more you can present a convincing attitude of "I am here to HELP," the more appreciative and interested they may be in bringing you on board. This is also true for pitching consulting assignments.

Your primary interest should be in learning "what needs to be done" (solving their need).

Focusing your comments and questions on how you can help, rather than on personal issues of what resources, office space, and other secondary issues, should help convince them that you are focused on them and their needs rather than on yours.

As you begin to satisfy them in the interview of your intentions on their behalf, the "fit" will improve and become comfortable for both you and them.

Once you have an offer, you can decide if the opportunity is a "fit" for you. But, until that point, ensure you have them and identifying and satisfying their needs 100% in mind.

CHAPTER 14

"I'm Here to Help" — Reduce the Risk of Them Hiring You

I work with executives of all ages across the country that have a range of job titles in a variety of industries, and the one common trait those in a 45-year old job search portray in their job search is that they sell themselves too aggressively.

Being "bright-eyed and bushytailed" was the right style when you were in your twenties and thirties. Employers sought energetic, ambitious prospective employees who they could train and mold into successful executives. So, "selling yourself" was what we all were told to do. And we did so with vigor . . . and success in most cases.

However, now that you are in your forties and fifties, over-selling yourself is 1) unnecessary and 2) wrong. At this point in your career, you must instead "insert yourself into the new position with confidence and tact" as one of my clients reflected recently.

She had been interviewing for a CMO position at several Bay Area firms with little success. Smart, well-educated and fresh from several successful start-ups, she had approached each new interview with the same high energy and take-charge attitude that she had developed during her 23-year marketing career.

When she then engaged my career strategy services, she was frustrated and gun-shy. "At each company, I was told that I was 'overqualified' for the position. I'm not sure what I'm doing wrong, but I need to figure it out soon."

In our meetings during which we thoroughly assessed her as an individual and executive, tightened up her resumé and created an engaging bio and other communications materials, I found myself often "bowled over" by her persona. It became clear that instead of presenting a profile of someone who would readily "fit into" the company and provide the right kind of leadership, her intense persona borne of years of success, had the potential effect of intimidating and sabotaging her candidacy.

We concluded that her being told by several companies that she was "overqualified" was "HR code" for believing she might be difficult to manage and might alienate her co-workers.

As I had seen this "overqualified" phenomenon many times in my work with clients, we agreed to adopt a more creative approach.

We agreed that she would begin to present a more "HELPFUL" approach in future interviews and portray herself as a strong team-leader and member, sensitive to developing good people, capable of nurturing good ideas with the help of others, and generally, interested in doing what the company needed to do to continue their success.

This shift from "I can do anything" that worked when she was younger and less experienced, to an attitude of "I'm here to help" was a critical, and as it turned out, a very effective tool in recent interviews.

She found people more interested in and comfortable with her, quickly engaging in more meaningful and informative interviews that will likely lead to an offer soon.

So, in any interactions now that you are over 45 years of age, consider approaching others with equanimity and quiet confidence rather than power and domination. You are now a pro and do not need to press your case as aggressively.

This "helpful" attitude will feel better and require less energy, which are good things as you mature in your career.

CHAPTER 15

Get the Job You Deserve, Not the One You Want

S peaking with a forty year-old job-seeker recently, he said in frustration, "I just cannot find the job I want."

Sound familiar?

We are often envious of certain jobs and professions that are much more appealing, lucrative, or exciting than the one we have or had. The job we "want" is very often elusive and, frankly, impossible to land.

I suspect a key reason this is true is that "getting the job you want" is not the correct objective. Identifying and successfully pursuing the "job you deserve" is the more appropriate, and in the end, the more successful approach.

Adopting the latter objective, *getting the job you deserve*, involves ignoring job boards, headhunter calls (however rare they may be), friends' suggestions and endless networking groupings. These and other sources will confuse and complicate your job search because most provide opportunities that do not represent jobs that you deserve. They are simply not right for you.

Instead, getting that "right job" involves your decision to adopt a proactive job/career search based on a fundamental belief that there are great jobs within thirty or forty miles of your home that you *deserve, not just want* — jobs that are totally congruent with you and your goals and those of the prospective company.

A job you deserve is a job that is responsive not only to your title, salary, location and other traditional job interests, but leverages and focuses on your personal needs, talents, and yes, your idiosyncrasies. You gain, they gain. This requires that you really know yourself. It requires that you understand your true interests (sales, creative, R&D, operations, etc.) thoroughly and your needs (team or solo work, close or remote supervision, general or personalized incentives, fast or deliberate decision-making environments, a traditional or non-traditional work environment, etc.) in depth.

This additional critical information provides you with insights into what jobs you deserve at companies where, for a range of solid reasons, you deserve to work. These are the jobs and companies in which you are likely to succeed, rather than just jobs you want or seem cool.

There are many professional assessment and career action plans available through experienced career coaches. To find the right one, interview local career coaches. The right career coach will ensure he/she has conducted the right individual and professional assessments that tightly define the characteristics of the right job for you. Use this checklist to evaluate positions and companies that appear right for you, ones that you deserve. Then, contact them and link your needs to their needs. That's how business works and that is how your job/career search should work.

CHAPTER 16

Interview for an Offer, Not Just a Job

Sounds strange, right? Most of us assume that the main purpose of interviewing is to get a job.

Not exactly!

Having coached dozens of mid and late-career executives across the country in the last ten years, *I believe that you are interviewing to get an offer, not necessarily a job*.

Think about it. How many times have you been seeking employment where the specific job is really not what you want, but the company is?

The point is that you should be interviewing to join the company in a position that makes sense for you, not simply a job that is listed on a job board or introduced to you by a zealous recruiter. You are seeking work that is right for YOU, not just a job.

The way to accomplish this is to get an offer. Then, once the company has committed to you with this offer, you are in the "catbird's seat." Up until the offer, you were one of many candidates. Therefore, you played ball and did your best in the interviewing process. Once you have a *written* offer in hand, it is now your turn to ask the probing questions, meet more people, visit a couple of company offices or whatever you need to do to convince yourself that this is the right place and job for you.

Then, meet with the hiring manager (not anyone else) and have an adult conversation regarding whether this offer is best for you and them, and discuss how you see revising it to better serve both parties.

In most cases, you will focus on the specific position in question and negotiate a better offer. They want you; this is the best time to ensure you get what you think you need to be properly rewarded and motivated to do your best for them. It is also the last chance you will get for a long time to realize your key demands and needs.

In a lot of cases, the job they offered is not quite right for you. This is the time to ask if they can revise the position or identify another role in the company more in sync with you and your goals. One of my clients recently convinced a financial services firm to combine two open marketing positions, which resulted in a VP title and more money.

Yes, this requires some courage and finesse. But, remember, with a firm offer, they have said, "We want you to join the company." It is now up to you to ensure that you will be doing "the right work for you," not just filling a position on an org. chart.

So focus on getting an offer, and then focus on shaping the actual job to best fit your talents and needs as well as being responsive to the company's requirements.

CHAPTER 17

Your Age and Risk/Reward in a Job Search

As an experienced advertising executive turned headhunter turned career strategist since 2002, I have been interested in the role of "risk and reward" in the job and career search process and how age affects these factors.

Numerous articles in recent years extol the value of learning to fail as part of becoming a strong executive and member of a company or consulting team. In past years, failure was avoided at all costs, but with the advent of more youthful executives succeeding more quickly in the worlds of finance, technology and other industries, companies have sought out job candidates who have failed, as well as succeeded in their careers.

This suggests to me that younger executives should be able to explain their mistakes and what they learned from them, so as to demonstrate learning and maturation along the way.

So in the first ten or fifteen years of your career, you should present yourself as a high-risk, high-reward candidate. "Hire me and I will apply my 'wins and losses' to building your business and helping your company succeed. We may hit some rough spots, but we will prosper from understanding and solving them."

The reverse is applicable, I believe, to executives 45 and older. In this case, you should reduce the perceived risk of hiring you. "Hire me and I won't disappoint you or upset the applecart."

Think about it. The company is considering you for a position in middle or upper management. They know you can do the job by reviewing your resumé. What they really want to know in the interview is what will you be like to work with? Will you work well with younger supervisors? Will you ascribe to the way the company does business or will you insist on bringing old ways to the new company? Will you be open to being one of the team as opposed to leading the charge when there are others in the lead position? In short, will you work out here?

So what should you do? Cool your jets! Listen to the questions in the interview with a third ear…what are they really asking of you? Respond with an attitude of "helping" rather than the attitude of the ambitious 27-year-old you used to be. Cast your answers in supportive as well as creative terms. They know you can DO the job; they really need to know HOW you will do the job.

So, REDUCE THE RISK of hiring you if you are 45-plus. Make it easy for them to take you on. Be part of the solution rather than the problem "can we manage him/her?" Be open to an initial consulting relationship, which gives you and the company a trial period of time, usually six months, to fall in love with each other (if it does not work out, as a consultant, they are a "client" on your resumé instead of a formal job). Make no demands beyond fair compensation and meaningful benefits. Stay on the subject of the job rather than bring up distractions that can negate your candidacy. Be your most likeable and supportive self. Get the offer! Then do your due diligence.

Make it easy to hire you if you are over 45. Reduce the risk.

Make it a bit of a risk to hire you if you are under 45. Increase the promise of a big reward for hiring you.

CHAPTER 18

How to Expand Your Job Search Network — Now!

A s you have learned in your job search, contacts and networking are perhaps the most effective tools to employ in finding and landing your next job.

Prior to 2001, jobs seemed to materialize in front of our eyes. Recruiters called frequently with enticing opportunities. Friends alerted you to openings at their companies. Even your local grocery checkout clerk seemed to have great job leads.

Of course, that is now history. Jobs, importantly, the job you "deserve" (as opposed to the job you "want" — but that is another subject) are elusive. Your job search now has to become totally proactive. You have to go after it. And to do so, you have to turn to your existing contacts for leads as well as expanding your list of helpful contacts.

So, here are several ways to quickly expand your network of potential job leads and how to reach out to them:

- ✓ **Create your "hit list" of companies within 30 miles** (45-minute commute) of your home that you believe you can help based upon your interests, experience, talents, and the nature of the company's business, the "match" between you and them. You should have about 10-20 of these companies about which you have learned everything including reading their website "press" section to learn what they are currently doing (this section provides hints as to how you can insert yourself into current business initiatives), and reading the bios of senior executives (to get a sense of the culture and any "connections" you may have with them).

✓ **Dive deeply into LinkedIn.** Go online and read tutorials regarding how to use LinkedIn to identify and reach out to likely suspects at companies on your "hit list" who could hook you into an opportunity at their company. Enter these names and contact info into an online database (freecrm.com is basic but useful) and begin to track all of your activities with each person.

✓ **For more potential contacts, look back in your career** for people who "sold to you" in your prior positions. These people tried to do business (and many probably did) with you and will remember you, and will very likely be willing to help you in your search. Add them to your database.

✓ **Reflect on all of your previous jobs** and identify people via LinkedIn that you have forgotten who could help you.

✓ **Check into professional group websites** for the names of members who could help. You may have to join the group to get access to this information, but joining appropriate groups is another way of staying abreast of developments in your industry.

✓ **Review your local Business Times** and other pertinent industry publications for the names of people with whom you should connect. Include editors and authors of articles that may be willing to turn you on to opportunities in their universe.

✓ **Go "all the way back" to your undergraduate** (and graduate) schools and forage through appropriate parts of their websites. Contact a few likely academicians who might love to connect you with their clients (as long as you do not represent a direct threat to those relationships).

✓ **Contact recruiters you know**. In addition to ensuring they know you are in the market, ask them for the names of executives they know in your industry that you should contact. This is in their self-interest, as you will obviously inform the people you contacted that "Phil Smith suggested you as someone who I should know in my job search." Remember, these days, everyone is conscious of the job search challenge and are more than likely willing to help you if you approach them in a "low-key fashion." Also, remember that you are someone of real value and expertise whom people will be pleased to meet.

✓ **That "low-key fashion" is simply a three-part email** (this is why I am writing, this is briefly who I am and how I am aligned with what your company is doing, and I would like to meet to learn more about how I might be able to contribute to your company's success). All they can do is say "no" or not respond. If the latter, do not give up.

✓ **Do not send your resumé. Send your one-page bio** with photo and contact info. A resumé says, "Help, I need a job." A bio says, "I am someone you may want to meet based on my terrific 'story'." If you do not have a bio, create one by referring to bios on websites you admire. Have a few people who know you edit your bio. Make a PDF of the final version so that it will "transmit" properly to various Windows and Mac computers.

✓ **Call these folks one week later to follow-up.** Refer to your email (date and time) should you reach them live and briefly state what you wrote in the email. Do not oversell yourself; keep it brief. Endeavor to engage them to the point that you both agree to meet or speak at more length right then.

✓ If you do not reach them, **leave a brief voicemail** referring to your email, re-state its contents and say you would love to hear from them. Also, state that you will call again (provide a specific day and time- before 9AM) and call them at that time.

Using your **database tracking,** call each person about every ten days and consider re-sending your email after about a month. Keep your outreach easy-going and focused. Remember, you are an expert in your field and it is to their benefit to meet you. They may be smart enough to also be building their network!

Continue to add prospective resources to your database and have confidence that you will make several very useful contacts in this fashion that will lead to getting the "job you deserve for career happiness and success."

Once you land that new job, take an hour or two every month to communicate with key members of our new network. Keep them abreast of your activities and offer your help should they require it at some point.

CHAPTER 19

"Lean Into"
Your Job Search

W
hat I like most about Sheryl Sandburg's career book is the title, *Lean In.*

During my many years in business, the most memorable people I have known are those who "leaned in," who pushed the pace of the relationship with tact.

I particularly admire the men and women who "leaned in thoughtfully," with class and a sense of urgency, but also of balance.

We are all trying to reach all sorts of people, be it customers, people on LinkedIn, recruiters, hiring executives, board members and other targets of our business and career-building activities.

Most of us are reticent to press ourselves on others. We think it is impolite or boorish. Others overdo their outreach and burnout their relationships before they even get started.

Leaning in and pushing the pace with balance is a tricky, but important, technique to develop.

From my view, the world is a much more competitive arena than in past years. Time is of the essence, jobs are fleeting, companies and people come and go. That requires that we become much more tactical and agile in our business-building and career-building activities. Everyone understands this now; everyone "gets the joke."

The "joke" is that we are constantly communicating one-to-one, by phone, tablet, laptop, etc., to make something happen. People understand that because they are doing the same thing.

So, now that you realize that everyone is in this self-promotional boat, you can start rowing yours faster. You can lean in more — you can push the pace with people, especially in your career search.

When you send an introductory email to meet someone (with your bio, NOT your resumé attached), leave them a voicemail a day later calling attention to your email with date/time and purpose in contacting them. Be brief, but clear in what you are seeking (a meeting, a reference, a lead, etc.). Then follow-up one day sooner than you are comfortable with (leaning in means being a little uncomfortable), and every few days a little sooner than you normally would until you achieve your objective.

If your reason for meeting them is legitimate — meaning that you have done your homework and you know what real value you could bring to the person or company you are contacting — then pushing the pace of getting to them is totally appropriate. As far as you are concerned, they NEED you, for very good reasons that you can readily describe.

At job fairs, professional mixers, local coffee shops and other venues of potential contacts and opportunity, don't fail to move out of your comfort zone and "lean into" the crowd. Shake hands firmly, look people in the eyes, smile, speak with sincerity, poise and knowledge. Ask them what they do, why they do it, how you might be able to help them. Briefly make them aware of those same factors on your behalf.

On phone calls, stand up, lean into the conversation, again with poise and balance. Be present. Push the pace. That is called energy. And people react well to energy, as long as it is not nuclear.

And in interviews, be present, aware, poised yet slightly intense. Lean into the conversation when appropriate to make a point, then relax a bit so that you do not take over the conversation.

Remember, Sheryl said, "lean in," not shout, boast, dominate or otherwise overwhelm the other person. We are speaking here about a balanced playing field between you and whomever you are speaking with.

Move a little out of your comfort zone. Lean in. Practice it!

CHAPTER 20

"Tell Me About Yourself"

T his is perhaps, the most critical question asked by interviewers. It is an easy icebreaker and it appears to be a pretty simple question at first blush.

But it is actually a hidden bomb, and often the person asking it does not realize this either.

The reasons it is a critical question and also a potential bomb is that you may respond by telling a lengthy, disjointed and totally useless story with no real beginning, middle or end. Unless you are alert and prepared for it, it will stop the interview in its tracks.

Usually, we answer the question by more or less reciting our resumé. Why do we do this? Because we have not properly prepared for the question. The interviewer does not need you to recite your resumé. It is right in front of him or her.

What they really want to know, and even they may not be keenly aware of this, is:

> What are you like to work with? How do you operate? Will we like you? Will you like us? Will you succeed here? Or fail?

So, when presented with this question, be prepared to answer in this fashion:

✓ "Well, thanks Bob, for that question right up front, because there are some key things about me that may not be on my resumé that I really want you to know about me.

✓ "Three key things come to mind. First, I am very interested in this position and believe that my experience, but more importantly, my primary interests lie in helping your company expand your distributor network and develop new services.

✓ "Secondly, I have been working in this arena for several years in my (current, past) positions, and am proud of my results in (define those results briefly in terms of numbers and percentages).

✓ "Third, one of my strengths is building new teams quickly to address new initiatives like this one at your company. Quiet leadership, consistent support of my people and sharing the hard work and hopefully, the rewards of a job well-done motivate me on a daily basis."

Wow! In two minutes or less, the interviewer has an attractive and energetic profile of you that is additive to your resumé and that summarizes it in clear terms of what they may be seeking in a successful candidate.

The interviewer sees your eyes come alive, your body sit up straighter, your voice become confident and just a bit urgent. You begin to become more than just a resumé and a name on their interview calendar.

You become a *solid candidate*, which is your goal.

CHAPTER 21

"You Are Overqualified"

Many of my older clients speak of how frustrating it is to hear this following a series of what appeared to be terrific interviews.

Here is what I think happened in those interviews and what may be happening in your interviews.

You *over-sold* yourself. You "leaned in" too far. The reason I have this section right after the two above is that, while I urge you to be prepared to present your candidacy in confident and attractive terms, I also believe you need to keep your energy a bit in check so as not to overwhelm the interviewer, especially if they are twenty years your junior.

Any company, and any executive interviewing you, is seeking the best possible person for the job. But, they are also human and view each candidate on the basis of not only *can they do the job* but *how will they do the job*.

If you are a large man or a tall, vibrant woman, you may very simply, scare the hell out of them — especially if you are going to report to them.

Moderate your posture without diluting your evident interest in the job. Provide concise, positive answers but avoid speaking too long. Present a "HELPING" attitude; convince them you are hear to support their efforts as opposed to bringing your team, ideas or personality to bear on the assignment prematurely. Ensure you are trying to learn why they are interviewing — what is the need. What is the problem that needs solving? And stick to explaining how you can help satisfy that need or problem.

Make it easy for them to hire you. Reduce the risk. Explain. Don't boast or over-explain. Keep things moderate and easy-going.

Everyone wants to hire "overqualified" people. They just want to avoid a bull in a china shop.

CHAPTER 22

Smile, Smile, Smile

This is particularly true the older you become. For whatever reason — or reasons — life seems to become a bit tougher and more complex and more challenging as we grow older.

That often results in our smiling less, unwittingly.

This lack of mirth and humanity, this dourness can upset folks and co-workers around us.

So, very simply, practice smiling.

And saying hello with good eye contact.

Look at people.

And smile.

Smile.

CHAPTER 23

Marketing Your "Subset" of Expertise

Lots of us seem to know our general area of expertise. We are engineers, accountants, sales people, copywriters, attorneys and other professional types.

Knowing your "supporting professional focus" can be very useful in identifying and obtaining the best position for yourself, and it is easily accomplished.

Look back in your professional and personal endeavors and think about the "role" you played on an engineering team, as a member of a corporate accounting team, as a member of a successful sales organization. Recall what "role" you typically played or were asked to play by others.

Did you organize the meetings, set the strategy, take the notes, run the budget numbers, come up with the creative solutions, write the policies and procedures or lead the entire effort? As a general subject expert, what is your *supporting expertise*?

It is that dual role that you should reflect in your resumé's "Objective" statement and in your Bio and other search documents, including introductory emails.

Example: "Highly-experienced corporate software developer at leading US and International Software Firms with unique ability to create profitable products based upon accurate cost projections and efficient product development procedures."

Now, the reader will know that you are 1) a seasoned software developer who can, 2) work effectively with the finance, marketing as well as other R&D professionals to successfully launch profitable software packages. If that is what they are seeking, you have made it clear that you are a potential candidate. If it is not what they are seeking, then you very likely do not want the job, as it is not "in your wheelhouse."

Take a look at your resumé and your biography and ensure that you have this key information in a prominent position. Also, it should be on your LinkedIn profile and at other locations where you are marketing yourself.

CHAPTER 24

The America's Cup as a Career Search Template

S an Francisco hosted the amazing America's Cup in **2013.** This world-class event brought the fierce competition for the oldest trophy in international sports back to the United States for the first time in 18 years. The rivalry between the top-notch crews began with extensive preparations among the contenders in full swing. Every aspect of each crew's preparedness was thoroughly examined, improved, refined and finely honed into an unmatched contender for the Cup. It was this attention to detail that finally carried the day — and made the difference — for the U.S. Team.

Your career deserves the same preparedness in order for you to "sail the best race." This requires an excellent Assessment of your "team" and a winning Action Plan to achieve your goal of career success.

The America's Cup teams assessed their team vision, sharpened their training and professional education programs, refined their financial plans to support their bid, applied the best of technology and design to yacht and rigging design and racing tactics, built their team's physical fitness levels and belief in themselves, and created their marketing and communications programs to tell their exciting story to build support among their country's fans. The teams made sure they included their families in these plans, as it was a long 28 months before the starting gun fired and the America's Cup was off in the lee of the Golden Gate Bridge.

Take a cue from these teams and take the same action with your "career team."

- ✓ First, assess yourself and your vision. Do you know yourself and your talents in detail? Do you have a clear idea of who you are, what you are best at, and where you are going? The answers to these and other critical questions must be clear in your mind before you try to take action with your career. Sailors chart courses to win races by knowing a great deal about the tides, winds, competition and other key factors. You have to do the same.

- ✓ Consider your educational and professional preparation for the future. Do you need to get an MBA or a professional qualification in your field to move ahead? Does your "career team" need key courses that you could obtain at a nearby college or university to improve your professional knowledge and candidacy?

- ✓ Are you in good financial condition? If you were to lose your current job or decide to change careers, how long could you support yourself on savings and investments?

- ✓ Are you well-equipped with the right technology support? Are you as hip as your peers in social media, personal computer skills and other prerequisites for life in the digital age?

✓ Are you healthy and fit, or do you need to take immediate action to lose fifteen pounds or get a physical to ensure your health can support your career activities?

✓ How is your spiritual life? Do you have faith in yourself? Do you have a good group of friends and peers to provide the energy and support you will need to forge ahead?

✓ Do you have a solid and persuasive personal marketing program? Have you created communications including a sharp, distinctive resumé, a powerful bio and 60-second elevator speech that separates you from the pack and causes people to want to meet and help you? Does your resumé summary paragraph explain who you are and what professional situations you are seeking in concise and memorable terms? When asked to "tell me about yourself," can you do so in a confident, precise and impressive fashion that causes the interviewer to realize how clear you are regarding your talents, interests and fit with their company?

✓ Last, but not least, like the America's Cup teammembers, are you including and involving your family in your preparations as well as your action steps? Keeping them in the loop will provide you with more energy and give them a sense of true teamwork — a nice thing!

So, look hard at yourself, your "career team" elements and assess them and address them with improvements, refinements, additions and deletions.

Then plot those next career steps, sail hard to each mark, round them with style and finesse, and drive to the finish line with a new job or industry role as the trophy for all your hard work and deliberate preparations.

CHAPTER 25

To Go Forward,
Look Back at Your Roots

O ne of the best techniques that I know in helping
my career coaching clients more clearly define
their true interests and talents is to suggest they sit
down during a quiet period, perhaps late at night, to consider and write about "their roots."

The use of various formal assessment tools, such as the
Birkman Method, Myers-Briggs and other well-regarded
tools, is very useful in identifying your strengths and the
areas of business in which you are likely to succeed.

A useful exercise to help guide your future career direction with actual experiential support information is to
"think back." Think back to what your teachers and other
"youth guides" said you were good at. Did they suggest
that you patiently studied your schoolwork, or that you
seemed to enjoy speaking to the class or that you were always the most organized kid in the class? Market research, general management or administrative careers
would be natural directions for each of these behaviors.

What did your friends always say about you? What did
your class yearbooks say were your noteworthy attributes? Were you the class clown? Perhaps sales is the right
place for you, building relationships through upbeat
means. Were you always surrounded by people or active

on sports teams? You may be right for leading technical or operational teams. Were you always coming up with novel school newspaper columns or writing term papers that got the approval of your teachers and fellow students? Maybe you should focus on creative careers such as becoming a technical or advertising copywriter.

When you examine your high school and college roots, what role did your team members on a class project always ask you to play? Was it a leadership role presenting the group's work, or was it an administrative role ensuring that everyone knew the date and time for the next group meeting? Did you always draw the pictures or handle the white board during discussions?

All of these recollections will help you identify your real-world talents and expertise, increasing your confidence in the direction you choose to undertake.

CHAPTER 26

These Days, We Are Always in a Job Search

The new reality of an executive career is that you should always be taking the necessary steps to advance your career. This dedication to doing the "career homework" applies to individuals who are employed, but seeking better or alternative careers, as well as for those who are out of work and seeking new employment.

As a Career Coach and Strategist, I work with executives at all stages of their careers. My clients are terrific when it comes to engaging themselves in the personal assessments I conduct to help them know themselves and their ideal career profile more deeply and intimately. And they are equally adept and motivated to work on improving their resumés, creating interesting bios that tell their stories in a compelling fashion, as well as tightening up their 60-second elevator speeches. They get their LinkedIn profiles updated, join LinkedIn groups, begin to identify networking contacts and join useful job boards.

However, when I ask them what they are *doing* about the challenging part of a career program, which is taking AC-TION by making new contacts, making calls and setting meetings to explore new horizons, they often have made very little progress.

So, I ask you: *What are you DOING* about:

✓ Reaching out to people with whom you have worked for leads and new ideas?

✓ Pulling together some people you admire for bi-weekly breakfast networking and career growth support sessions?

✓ Identifying ten companies where you "deserve to work" within thirty miles of your home and contacting key executives (from LinkedIn or their website) for exploratory talks?

✓ Reaching out to target company *board members* who are very influential and open to being contacted, especially if you share something in common?

✓ In the same vein, re-contacting influential teachers with whom you got along and who might know of corporate or consulting opportunities in industries of interest to you?

✓ Contacting carefully selected retained search partners whose backgrounds and search focus mirror yours?

✓ Suggesting to those key recruiters that they can contact you if they feel you can HELP them with any of their searches in your area of expertise (and tell them again what that is)?

✓ Keeping your family and friends who are concerned for you well informed of your progress?

✓ Carefully tracking your activities with CRM software to ensure nothing drops through the cracks?

✓ Updating your references to ensure they are current and supportive of your candidacy should you identify an exciting new opportunity?

In short, doing your homework (better resumé, powerful bio, well-researched target company list, etc.) is important, but success will be achieved through WHAT YOU ARE DOING each and every day to support your career objectives.

CHAPTER 27

What Others Think of You
Is None of Your Business

S ounds crazy, right? Well, like my coaching advice in "Interview for the Company, Not the Job" and "Why Not Contact Board Members in Your Search?," this non-traditional career search idea makes sense.

Many of us are trained marketers. Just as we have learned how to sell products and services for our employers or consulting clients, we have also learned that we have to effectively market ourselves.

We have done all the right things. We have written our own Communications Platforms (key message, target audience, support points and 4-5 stories that support our candidacy) and then revised our resumés and written interesting bios and 60-second elevator speeches. We have created catchy selling lines for our websites and our business cards and in some cases, handed out coffee cups to brand ourselves. We have done everything possible to shape others' opinions of ourselves and to position ourselves for new opportunities.

And then we find that people forget what we do for a living, fail to contact us when they have a problem to solve that we would handle in a minute, draw a blank when they are called as a reference for us and simply, don't seem to know us after all that work. Even our own mothers ask, "What is it that you do?"

So we wonder and agonize over why this is often the case. Why don't people call? Why doesn't the HR person call me back for another interview? Why didn't a board member at XYZ Company (where I really deserve to work!) respond to my very clever email? Why didn't my friendly headhunter (who I have helped numerous times!) call me regarding a search I know she has that is so perfect for me?

Wonder, wonder, wonder. Worry, worry, worry. All it does is cause you to lose sleep and irritate your loved ones.

Realize, please, that you can only do so much about marketing yourself and impressing your profile and goals on others. Do your best and then leave it to the gods and move on to another opportunity or activity that offers promise.

Frankly, others probably think you're terrific. They are just spending most of their time on their own careers and jobs, and all the work it takes to keep them alive and growing.

CHAPTER 28

Acknowledgement —
the Secret to Success

I n my Career Strategy Coaching practice, I have learned that most of my clients are quite consumed with their job or career search, almost to the exclusion of thinking of others. This is intriguing as "others" and their regard and support for you, are key to success in your life and career.

I read a posting by another career coach recently that I liked. He suggested that instead of saying your name first when meeting someone, ask for their name first. "Hi, what's your name?" or, "Hi, what brings you to this event?" is about them, not you. Acknowledging others first and foremost, rather than being self-focused, will be more effective, productive and memorable. Acknowledging others by thanking them for an idea or help via email or a note, being sure to say a sincere hello to a receptionist or a store clerk, and smiling with your mouth and your eyes upon meeting a new acquaintance establishes that *you are about them, not just about yourself.*

CHAPTER 29

What to Do When You Don't Get the Job Offer

In my many years of coaching mid and late-career executives to seek "rewarding work, not just a job," I have been mystified by an almost universal response on the part of candidates when they are rejected in favor of another executive for a position they really desired.

These executives, who are highly qualified, talented and motivated, simply "take no for an answer" and move on to other opportunities.

What a waste of weeks of work on their part interviewing for the position as well as the contacts they made at the subject company, many or most of which were likely to have been positive ones.

Should you be rejected for a job, my earnest advice to you is the following:

1. If you really wanted the position, express that fact and the reasons for your interest in a follow-up letter or email to all the people you met. State in a pleasant, yet confident fashion that you would like to stay in touch and hope they will reach out to you should other opportunities arise in the near future.

2. Specifically follow-up in a phone call with executives you met in the process with whom you really "hit it off." Express your pleasure at having met them, remind them of your ongoing interest, and ask that they keep you in mind for future opportunities at the company or elsewhere. Add them to your LinkedIn contacts. LinkedIn will advise you when they have changed positions or companies — another reason for contacting them again.

3. Review the entire interviewing process in your mind (and with trusted advisors or your career coach) and endeavor to refine your interviewing skills and improve your professional presentation based upon any insights you can identify or glean from the people you met.

4. Add these people to your network and periodically update them on your progress (especially when you land a new job).

5. Consider offering to work in a consulting capacity if you are aware that the winning candidate may have more on their hands in the new position than they can handle.

6. Consider contacting the hiring executive or Human Resources in five months or so. Often the winning candidate will have succeeded or failed by this point, so your follow-up could be well timed.

7. Look for other ways to stay on their radar. Don't just let them "go away" if you were strongly interested in the company.

CHAPTER 30

Your Personal Target Company List: The Killer Tool

In this era of uncertain employment longevity, you would imagine that every savvy business person, employed or seeking new employment, would have a list of companies where they want to do business or get a job clearly in mind.

We call this your Target Company List. These are companies where you "deserve to work." You are seeking work at these companies, not just a job.

Recently I was presenting my "Non-Conventional Job Search Tips" class to a group of 45-plus (for the most part) job seekers at a community-sponsored career center in the San Francisco Bay Area. Now, this is an employment market that fortunately for those who reside here, is a hotbed of job opportunities due to the explosive growth of social media and biotech companies, as well as those industries that feed these voracious companies.

I asked how many folks, of the forty or so gathered in the room, had developed a list of target companies where they wanted to work, in fact, where they deserved to work.

Only two hands went up! Everyone in the group had their resumés, bios, 60-second elevator speeches, websites, LinkedIn pages and other tools in good shape. But, they were lacking their most important tool, a *target company list*.

My job search coaching practice has three parts: self-assessment, action plan development and then the all-important third step, action plan execution. The key component of the job search execution phase is compiling a list of ten to twenty companies within thirty miles of your home (keep the commute sane) where you believe you should be working. The companies should meet your job criteria (that's another subject) and you should feel you are a match with their mission as stated on their websites (check the homepage, press releases, bios, etc. to learn what the company is trying to accomplish).

In brief, you are interviewing for the company, not the specific job. The job is momentary; the company is for the long-term.

Then, via LinkedIn and Lead.411 and other sites offering information about these companies, you create a list of executives, past and present, and then reach out to them via email and voicemail.

Your approach is simple: "This is why I am contacting you (I like the new xyz program you are developing), why I may be of interest to you (I have worked on xyz for five years with great results at ABC companies), and I WANT TO MEET YOU." The worst that can happen is nothing. The best is that they respond.

Using this simple method, a recent client emailed the CEO of a major insurance company regarding his interest in joining their training team. He got a response in two days and has been in conversations (this is important — conversations, not interviews) with them.

This was a "cold outreach" that he turned into a very "hot outreach" because he was able to connect the company and himself in three brief paragraphs in an email sent to a decision maker gleaned from LinkedIn.

This takes some hard work and thinking, but it is well worth the effort, I promise.

Having a target list of companies with whom you want to do business or obtain employment/consulting and then reaching out in brief, targeted emails to key executives is the best business-building or job-seeking tactic I know of.

Try it. Today. And keep at it. Begin a proactive outreach program today to YOUR TARGET COMPANY LIST.

CHAPTER 31

Your "Inner Career Coach"

I have been coaching college grads and executives around the country since 2004 in my own practice after thirty years in advertising management and retained executive search. During that time, I have noted the explosive growth of coaching across a range of subjects: health, career, relationships, social media, etc. This surge of demand for coaches is somewhat bewildering, and I think a bit over-used in many cases.

In general, most of us know what we ought to be doing for ourselves, our families, our jobs and our careers. We just do not listen to our "inner coach." Instead, we resort to outside help, believing that we really need another person in order to figure it all out.

As a coach, my practice is designed to help people do a better job at successfully pursuing their careers. However, I sometimes get the feeling that they think I am going to do the heavy lifting for them. This is the same feeling I used to have as a retained search executive. Candidates would come to our office assuming we were there to find them a job. Not so. We were there to satisfy our clients' needs for great executives.

The fact is that coaches, recruiters and other human resources professionals are there to guide people and to help them. But, the individual has to do the hard self-assessment, career planning and plan implementation work themselves. Anything less is sure to fail.

Self-understanding and reality testing are critical to being successful. Relying primarily on yourself is critical to being successful. Judiciously hiring coaches is a good idea, but it must be seen as augmenting your efforts, not replacing them.

So, rely on your "inner coach." Listen to that coach. Spend quiet time taking notes, understanding what works for you and what does not. Where do you *deserve* to work, not *want* to work? What types of people and working environments are best for you and which ones should you avoid? What types of companies and executives within those companies *need you?* What is the most effective way to approach them and attract their attention? Your inner coach will provide a great many of those answers.

Once you have done the hard thinking, it may be time to engage a professional coach to help you clarify, refine, and express your candidacy in an excellent resumé and bio. The coach's job should be to encourage, guide and refine your thinking rather than do it all for you. Hopefully, the result will be a faster, more successful career search process at a greatly reduced cost to you in time and money.

CHAPTER 32

Get In Shape for Your Career Search

In my career coaching practice working with executives at all levels across the country, I address the entire person, not just their career or job objectives and concerns.

This includes getting lots of information and insights regarding their financial, spiritual, interpersonal relationships, family, education, hobbies and other important life issues.

Regarding a successful job search or career redirection, I think that the most important life issue to immediately address and solve is your health. Many of my clients are 45-plus. It is quite surprising to learn how some of them have not taken good care of themselves. They have tried to address all of the life issues above with varying degrees of success, but have neglected to have regular physicals and most importantly, get in shape.

Getting in great physical shape is critical to a successful job search or career redirection. Many people say to me that they are "too old" to get a new job or change their stripes. My response is that your age equals sagacity. You are now an expert, and should promote yourself on that basis.

What people really mean when they make the age comment, is that they LOOK too old; they are overweight and out of shape. Hiring executives are not going to be keen on hiring someone who does not appear to value their health and appearance. If you cannot take care of yourself, how will you be expected to take care of your job?

One of my clients took the mission of improving his health to heart. In a matter of months he lost forty pounds. More importantly, he kept his weight at the new level through a committed program of regular exercise and healthy dieting.

He looks ten years younger than his 54 years and is happier with himself than he has been in years. His wife is thrilled. He is also a candidate for several excellent senior executive positions that fit his career planning goals.

Look in the mirror. Do you look youthful, vigorous and healthy? If not, make a decision to lose weight and improve your overall health. Today.

CHAPTER 33

Look for the "No" in a Job and Career Search

L ooking for the "no" in a job or career search may seem like an odd objective, but consider this:

The sooner you determine, either from initial research of the company you are considering or in the interviewing process, that it is not the right company for you, the sooner you can move on to more productive opportunities.

Too many people lose momentum and precious time in their job search by spending too much time pursuing companies that are simply not right for them. And they know this. The problem is that they do not know what else to do. They assume that interviewing a lot is what they are supposed to be doing.

No, they should be interviewing only with companies that are right for them based on careful analysis and investigation.

You are not seeking a series of lukewarm "yes's;" you are seeking clarity by looking for the "no's" — the verbal and non-verbal signals that clearly indicate a red light for you with a particular company.

Rely on both your intellect and your "gut" to listen for the no's as well as indications, the yes's, that this could be the right place for you. If the no's outnumber the yes's, move on with other options with finesse and energy.

Don't waste time chasing rainbows because it makes you feel busy. Instead, examine each opportunity with a ruthless eye and focus only on those with brightly shining green lights.

CHAPTER 34

Why Not Call Board Members as Part of Your Search?

In your career search, consider contacting *board members*. Think about it. No one ever calls board members! They are not contacted by job seekers because people don't think to do so, or they are intimidated from doing so.

Board members are people too! They like to hear from smart, experienced executives like you who might be a solution to a problem or need that they have identified for their company. Board members have skin in the game and may be disgruntled with current executives or may be responsible for a major company initiative for which they may need your help.

Look up the board members of companies where you want to work and deserve to work based upon your skills, background and interests. Email them and call them, offer to meet to chat about the company and how you might be able to help. A hint as to what may be high on their minds could be found in the "Press" section of the company website. See if current projects, introductions, acquisitions or other news is right in your wheelhouse.

Contact board members. It could be a fast means of connecting with your target companies' key opportunities.

CHAPTER 35

Maintain a
Positive Attitude

L osing a job, being in an unhappy or unproductive
job, or simply dealing with a sluggish career path
can be very trying.

Just as an animal can "smell" a weakened prey, people
around you will quickly sense that you are hurting, angry
or dismayed, and will find it difficult to lend a hand, no
matter how much they want to.

An important aspect of seeking a new job, a new career or
pursuing anything "new" in your professional world is
your attitude. It has to be a positive one.

One way to adopt a positive attitude, and actually *feel* positive, is to do the things I discussed earlier in this book. Do
your self-examination, set your goals, create your action
plan and take a proactive approach to making good things
happen for you.

Other tools include forming a support group, getting
some training in aspects of your candidacy that may be
weaker than they should be. Consider getting some personal counseling to examine yourself in detail and consider obtaining a professional career coach to help develop
and guide your search. Join a gym and lose weight and
tone yourself. If you are already going to a gym, take it

more seriously and increase the challenge of your workout program.

If you find yourself "fighting" the fact of unemployment or under-employment, or are simply feeling like you are treading water, seek help from friends and professionals.

A great book to read is *Tech Grief: Survive and Thrive Through Career Losses* by Linda Donovan and Denise Kalm. They offer great insights and solutions to dealing with the fears, anger and dismay that are often associated with a career shock.

CHAPTER 36

Bringing it all Together!

As you have learned in your job search, contacts and networking are perhaps the most effective tools to employ in finding and landing your next job.

Prior to 2001, jobs seemed to materialize in front of our eyes. Recruiters called frequently with enticing opportunities. Friends alerted you to openings at their companies. Even your local grocery checkout clerk seemed to have great job leads.

Of course that is now history. Jobs, importantly, the jobs you deserve (as opposed to the jobs you want, but that is another subject), are elusive. Your job search now has to become totally proactive. You have to go after it. And to do so, you have to turn to your existing contacts for leads as well as expanding your list of helpful resources.

So, here are several ways to quickly expand your network of potential job leads and how to reach out to them:

- ✓ **Create your "hit list" of companies within 30 miles** (45-minute commute) of your home that you believe you can help based upon your interests, experience, talents, and the nature of the company's business, the "match" between you and them. You should have about 10-20 of these companies about which you have learned everything including reading their website "press" section to learn what they are currently doing (this section provides hints as to how you can insert yourself into current business initiatives), and reading the bios of senior executives (to get a sense of the culture and any "connections" you may have with them).

✓ **Dive deeply into LinkedIn.** Go online and read tutorials regarding how to use LinkedIn to identify and reach out to likely suspects at companies on your "hit list" who could hook you into an opportunity at their company. Enter these names and contact info into an online database (freecrm.com is basic but useful) and begin to track all of your activities with each person.

✓ **For more potential contacts, look back in your career** for people who "sold to you" in your prior positions. These people tried to do business with you (and many probably did) will remember you and will very likely be willing to help you in your search. Add them to your database.

✓ **Reflect on all of your previous jobs** and identify people via LinkedIn that you have forgotten who could help you.

✓ **Check into professional group websites** for the names of members who could help. You may have to join the group to get access to this information, but joining appropriate groups is another way of staying abreast of developments in your industry.

✓ **Review your local Business Times** and other pertinent industry publications for the names of people with whom you should connect. Include editors and authors of articles that may be willing to turn you on to opportunities in their universe.

✓ **Go "all the way back" to your undergraduate** (and graduate) schools and forage through appropriate parts of their websites. Contact a few likely academicians who might love to connect you with their clients (as long as you do not represent a direct threat to those relationships).

✓ **Contact recruiters you know**. In addition to ensuring they know you are in the market, ask them for the names of executives they know in your industry that you should contact. This is in their self-interest, as you will obviously inform the people you contacted that "Phil Smith suggested you as someone who I should know in my job search." Remember, these days everyone is conscious of the job search challenge and are more than likely willing to help you, if you approach them in a low-key fashion. Also, remember that you are someone of real value and expertise whom people will be pleased to meet.

✓ **That "low-key fashion"** is simply a three-part email (this is why I am writing, this is briefly who I am and how I am aligned with what your company is doing, and I would like to meet to learn more about how I might be able to contribute to your company's success). All they can do is say "no" or not respond. If the latter, do not give up.

✓ **Do not send your resumé.** Send your one-page bio with photo and contact info. A resumé says, "Help, I need a job." A bio says, "I am someone you may want to meet based on my terrific 'story." If you do not have a bio, create one by referring to bios on websites you admire. Have a few people who know you edit your bio. Be sure it "transmits" properly to various Windows and Mac computers during this editing process, and when final, make a PDF that can be easily emailed, no matter what the computer platform.

✓ **Call these folks one week later to follow-up**. Refer to your email (date and time) should you reach them live and briefly state what you wrote in the email. Do not oversell yourself; keep it brief. Endeavor to engage them to the point that you both agree to meet or speak at more length right then.

✓ If you do not reach them, leave a brief voicemail referring to your email, re-state its contents and say you would love to hear from them. Also, state that you will call again (provide a specific day and time before 9AM) and call them at that time.

✓ **Using your database tracking system**, call each person about every ten days and consider re-sending your email after about a month. Keep your outreach easy-going and focused. Remember, you are an expert in your field and it is to their benefit to meet you. They may be smart enough to also be building their network!

✓ **Continue to add prospective resources** to your database and have confidence that you will make several very useful contacts in this fashion that will lead to getting the "job you deserve for career happiness and success."

✓ **Once you land that new job,** take an hour or two every month to communicate with key members of your new network. Keep them abreast of your activities and offer your help should they require it at some point.

✓ Also, be sure to **thank people** who played an active role in your search.

CHAPTER 37

Your New Year's Career Search Resolutions (good anytime of the year)

Take some quiet time this month to consider where you are in your career and promise yourself to take specific action steps to re-affirm your current direction or begin to move into a totally new field of endeavor.

Consider these resolutions:

1. Most importantly, **I will do some self-assessment work** on my own or with a career coach to clearly define and understand who I am, why I am that way, and what I truly need in a job and a career.

2. **I will re-create "my story"** so that I can confidently answer that famous question "tell me about yourself" with focus, brevity, and energy. This step will help me clarify my career objectives and create an effective and vital career search action plan resulting in the right new position or new career for me I will "look for rewarding work, not just a job."

3. **I will ensure that my resumé is current**, no more than two pages in length and proofread

with a powerful two to three line summary statement at the top of the first page that defines my professional focus and what I am seeking. I will ensure that my bio is current and interesting to read and will cause someone to like and want to meet me.

4. I will ensure my **sixty-second "elevator speech" is brief and as interesting as my bio**. I will practice delivering it for my search until it is second nature. It will contain a memorable "button" about me (beekeeper, recently published author, ski champ, etc.).

5. **I will re-contact my references** (three supervisors/managers, three peers, three direct reports) to update them on my career search status, remind them of my key strengths, and thank them for being willing to act as a reference. I will avoid overusing my references and thank them when I "land" in my next chapter. At that point, I will also thank everyone who helped me.

6. **I will create or reenergize my support network** and meet them and new contacts on a weekly or biweekly basis.

7. **I will create a CRM file** (freecrm.com) and keep a careful record of all contacts that I have ever made that are pertinent to my career search. I will follow-up on all opportunities with alacrity and energy.

8. **I will draw a 30-mile circle around my home (45-minute commute) and identify all the companies** in that circle where I "deserve to work" based on a match between my profile and the company's profile. I will learn all that I

can via the Internet and my contacts about how their business could benefit from my expertise, skills and interests. I will contact the most likely executives, including *board members*, to establish relationships that might lead to consulting or employment.

9. **I will consider obtaining presentation skills and interview training** to sharpen my presence and confidence in interviews. I will prepare for the wide range of questions that I will be asked. I will be expert in how to interview effectively by phone or in person.

10. **I will dedicate a specific amount of time** each week, ideally the same days and times, **to my career search**. I will treat my search as seriously as I do (did) my job.

11. **If I am not working, I will find a part-time job** that keeps me feeling active, pays something, and is consistent in some way with my career objectives if possible.

12. **I will keep my family, friends, and support group current** regarding my career search and I will enlist their support and love to keep me energized and focused.

13. **Once I land that next consulting or full-time employment, I will thank those who helped** and I will keep doing all of the above to be well-prepared for the next "work interruption" or career shift.

Remember, jobs are fleeting; work is eternal.

Helpful Resources in No Particular Order that Should Be of Value to Your Career Search Process

Think and Grow Rich by Napoleon Hill. The classic guide to business and career success. A must on every executive's bookshelf.

What Color is Your Parachute by Richard Bowles. The "daddy" of career guides, it remains a seminal guide to pursuing the right job for you.

A Plan for Life by Eric Wentworth. Valuable information and guidance on health, career, love, wealth and other key aspects of a vigorous and rewarding life.

Tech Grief: Survive and Thrive Through Career Losses by Linda Donovan and Denise Kalm. A sensitive look at the often under-stated and debilitating aspects of the pain of transition.

Happiness: The Art of Living with Peace, Confidence and Joy by Douglas A. Smith. A warm and personal account by a top marketer. This is a 21st Century *Walden*.

Book Yourself Solid by Michael Port. A New York Times bestseller focused on salespeople, but valuable advice to apply to your job and career search.

The Contrarian Effect by Michael Port. You will notice numerous contrarian ideas about searching for your next job and managing your career in my book. This book provides others.

Just Listen by Mark Goulston. Great advice on how to contact "tough-to-reach" people to make a difference in your life. This concept is key to a career and job search.

The Pursuit of Wow! by Tom Peters. You have to be unique, committed and dynamic in your self-promotion. The famed Tom Peters provides numerous insights to consider and act upon.

Reinventing Yourself and *50 Ways to Create Great Relationships* by Steve Chandler. Powerful ways to connect and establish important and valuable life-long relationships and make critical improvements to your career and life.

Do the Work and *The War of Art* by Steven Pressman. Written by a former ad man and novelist, these books address the hard work that must be done to overcome the challenges facing all of us in our personal pursuits of happiness and satisfaction.

Other Important Resources:

Birkman Method Personality Assessment. www.birkman.com. The most comprehensive self-assessment tool provides your primary profile, and critical information regarding your needs and interests that drive your behavior. This information gives you the ability to effectively direct your career and explain where and why you are headed in a specific career direction and what jobs fulfill that mission.

linkedin.com .Has rapidly become the site of choice for gaining information in a job search and pursuing posted jobs. A must for every executive and job seeker- ensure your posting is complete, accurate and interesting.

lead411.com. Daily job leads customized to your location and objectives.

indeed.com. Largest jobs site; useful for interviewing skills and other job-related information

monster.com. A large and interesting job search website.

dice.com. Noted for its vibrant technology job search experience.

usajobs.gov. Provides information regarding government openings.

Marketing Executive Network Group (mengonline.com) and **Financial Executive Marketing Group (thefeng.org)**. Provide extensive professional industry information useful in a job search.

. . . AND MOST IMPORTANTLY,

Your family, your friends, your associates, your health, your energy, your spirit, your education, your character and your freedom. Value and utilize them all. — carefully and consistently!

ABOUT THE AUTHOR

PETER ENGLER has been a New York and San Francisco-based advertising agency executive leading ad campaigns for Clorox, SONY, Hunt-Wesson, Iomega and other leading products. He also held the position of VP Marketing at Citibank as well as at an early interactive television company, and was a retained senior executive recruiter at a top San Francisco search firm. He led the senior executive transition practice at a major outplacement firm, and since 2004, has operated his executive career coaching/strategizing and CEO/Executive Team-building practice. He has worked with executives at all points in their careers, across the country, with the simple objective of helping them "find rewarding work, not just a job," and has guided small and large team-building engagements with exciting results.

In addition to this book, he has authored his first novel, *New and Improved! A Political Thriller* about an ex-Navy combat pilot and NYC "Mad Man" who is hired to write a Presidential re-election campaign in 1992 and discovers a long-simmering plot to assassinate the President after Election Day. Ben Coleman has to resort to his courage and creative instincts to counter this diabolical plot and rescue the Presidency, and the country, from sure disaster.

Available on Amazon in Print and Kindle versions.

Engler Career Group • San Francisco, California
415-601-2444 • englercareergroup.com

IN CLOSING,

I hope this book has provided you with some new information and more importantly, a renewed commitment to do something really important for yourself. "Find rewarding work, not just a job."

Thanks for spending time with my book and your career. Helping people do a better job of strategizing their goals, building their career search tools and aggressively going after the right job for them is my passion.

I hope it becomes yours, too.

As I am a Career Strategist and Coach by profession and belief, I would be more than glad to have a phone conversation with you regarding your career or job search issues. I love this work and have had many successful engagements with people just like you.

Please feel free to email or call me (contact information follows) for a free twenty-minute consultation regarding your situation.

Good luck and happy hunting!

Peter G. Engler
Belvedere, California

englercareergroup.com
highperformanceexec.com
granthampress.com
415-601-2444
englercareergroup@gmail.com

P.S. If you like this book, I hope you will write a review of it on Amazon. Just go to my Author Central page here: http://amazon.com/author/peterengler, click on *Your Crystal Clear Career Path* on that page, scroll down to the reviews section and select the button to add your review. Thanks very much.

Made in the USA
San Bernardino, CA
07 May 2016